Appetizers
& Party Snacks

Microwave cooking times are approximate due to numerous variables, such as the microwave oven rated wattage, starting temperature, shape, amount, depth of food, etc. Use the cooking times as a guideline and check doneness before adding more time. Lower wattage ovens may consistently require longer cooking times.

OPENING ACT

Mussels, Tomatoes and Roasted Peppers

2 tablespoons olive oil
1 medium onion, finely chopped
3 cloves garlic, minced
1 pound tomatoes, coarsely
    chopped
    Dry white wine

1 large bay leaf
1 teaspoon salt
    Black pepper
1 jar (7 ounces) Italian-style
    roasted peppers
4 dozen mussels, scrubbed,
    debearded

Heat oil in large kettle over medium-high heat. Add onion and garlic; cook until softened, stirring frequently. Add tomatoes, 2 cups wine, the bay leaf, salt and black pepper to taste. Reduce heat to low; simmer, stirring occasionally.

Meanwhile, process roasted peppers with liquid in blender or food processor until pureed. Add to tomato mixture. Cook about 30 minutes, stirring occasionally. Add additional wine if mixture becomes dry. Increase heat to medium-high. Arrange mussels on tomato mixture. Cook, covered, until mussels open. Discard any mussels that do not open after 5 or 6 minutes. Remove mussels and discard top shell of each mussel. Return mussels to sauce. Discard bay leaf. Serve hot. Makes 8 appetizer servings.

Sesame Pork Appetizers

1½ pounds pork tenderloin
½ cup plus 1 tablespoon dry
  sherry, divided
⅓ cup plus 1 tablespoon soy
  sauce, divided
½ cup honey
½ cup sesame seeds
1 tablespoon sesame oil
1 clove garlic, crushed
½ teaspoon grated fresh ginger
1 green onion, finely chopped
  Spinach leaves

Place pork in large plastic bag.
Combine ½ cup of the sherry and 1
tablespoon of the soy sauce; pour over
pork, turning to coat. Tie bag.
Marinate in refrigerator 1 to 2 hours,
turning several times. Remove pork
from marinade. Spread honey on
plate. Spread sesame seeds in shallow
dish. Roll pork in honey, then in
sesame seeds. Arrange pork on
roasting rack set in roasting pan.
Bake at 350°F 25 to 30 minutes or
until meat thermometer registers
155°F. Let stand 5 minutes. Slice
thinly on the diagonal. Set aside.

Combine remaining ⅓ cup soy sauce,
remaining 1 tablespoon dry sherry,
the sesame oil, garlic, ginger and
onion in small bowl. Place bowl in
center of serving platter. Surround
the bowl with spinach leaves. Arrange
pork slices on top. Makes 10 to 12
appetizer servings.

Favorite recipe from **National Pork
Producers Council**

Marinated Tortellini with Vegetables

1 package (9 ounces) cheese-
  filled tortellini, cooked,
  drained
1 red bell pepper, cut into 1-inch
  pieces
1 green bell pepper, cut into
  1-inch pieces
½ pound small mushrooms
½ cup olive oil
¼ cup white wine vinegar
2 tablespoons chopped parsley
2 cloves garlic, minced
1 teaspoon dried basil, crushed
1 teaspoon dried oregano,
  crushed
1 teaspoon salt
  Black pepper

Combine tortellini, bell peppers and
mushrooms in medium bowl; set
aside. For marinade, combine oil,
vinegar, parsley, garlic, basil, oregano,
salt and black pepper to taste in small
jar with tight-fitting lid; shake until
well blended. Pour marinade over
tortellini and vegetables. Toss gently
to combine. Refrigerate, covered, up
to 24 hours. Before serving, bring to
room temperature. Makes 6 appetizer
servings.

Sesame Pork Appetizers

Spinach Pasta with Gorgonzola Dolcelatte® Sauce

Spinach Pasta with Gorgonzola Dolcelatte® Sauce

   4 ounces Gorgonzola Dolcelatte®
   ⅓ cup milk
   3 tablespoons butter
   ⅓ cup whipping cream
   8 ounces spinach noodles or
       shells, hot cooked, drained
   ⅓ cup freshly grated Parmigiano-
       Reggiano

Allow Gorgonzola to soften at room temperature for 30 minutes. Combine Gorgonzola, milk and butter in medium saucepan. Cook over low heat until smooth, stirring constantly. Add cream. Cook until hot and smooth, stirring constantly. Remove from heat. Pour sauce over pasta. Toss to coat. Add Parmigiano-Reggiano. Mix well. Serve with additional Parmigiano-Reggiano. Makes 8 appetizer servings.

Beef and Pistachio Pâté

   6 ounces sliced beef bacon
   ½ cup finely chopped onion
   3 cloves garlic, minced
   2 tablespoons butter or margarine
   2 pounds lean ground beef
   ½ cup fresh bread crumbs
   ⅓ cup shelled pistachio nuts
   ¼ cup snipped parsley
   2 tablespoons brandy
   1 egg, beaten
   1½ teaspoons salt

¾ **teaspoon dried thyme, crushed**
½ **teaspoon pepper**
⅛ **teaspoon ground nutmeg**

Line bottom and sides of 9×5-inch pan with bacon; reserve 4 slices. Cook and stir onion and garlic in butter in medium skillet over medium-high heat 3 minutes; cool. Combine ground beef, onion mixture, bread crumbs, nuts, parsley, brandy, egg, salt, thyme, pepper and nutmeg in large bowl; mix lightly but thoroughly. Press mixture firmly into bacon-lined pan; cover with reserved bacon. Set pan in 11¾×7½-inch baking dish on lowest rack of oven. Pour 1 quart boiling water into dish. Bake at 350°F 1½ hours. Remove pan from water. Fit another pan directly on top of pâté; add 3 pounds of weight (canned goods) and let rest 3 hours in cool place. Refrigerate, covered, 24 hours. Remove top bacon; invert and slice. Makes 8 to 10 appetizer servings.

Favorite recipe from **National Live Stock and Meat Board**

Antipasto

2 **anchovy fillets, finely chopped**
½ **cup CRISCO® Oil**
2 **tablespoons lemon juice**
3 **tomatoes, cut into wedges**
8 **lettuce leaves**
1 **jar (6 ounces) marinated
    artichoke hearts, drained**
8 **slices Italian salami**
4 **thin slices prosciutto or ham,
    cut into halves**
1 **can (6½ ounces) tuna, drained,
    separated into chunks**
8 **radishes**
8 **ripe olives**
  Capers, drained (optional)
  Parsley (optional)
  Salt (optional)
  Pepper (optional)

For dressing, place anchovies in small bowl; mash with fork. Add oil; stir in lemon juice. Place tomato wedges in another small bowl. Add 1 to 2 tablespoons of the dressing; toss to coat. Line large serving platter with lettuce leaves. Arrange tomatoes, artichoke hearts, salami, prosciutto, tuna, radishes and olives on lettuce. Sprinkle with capers, parsley, salt and pepper. Serve with remaining dressing. Makes 8 appetizer servings.

Antipasto

Apple-Beer Cheese Soup

    3 tablespoons butter or margarine
    ½ small onion, minced
    3 tablespoons all-purpose flour
    1¼ cups chicken broth
    ¾ cup unsweetened applesauce
    1 can (12 ounces) beer, at room
        temperature
    ⅛ teaspoon freshly grated or
        ground nutmeg
    ⅛ teaspoon white pepper
        Dash Worcestershire sauce
        Salt
    1 cup (4 ounces) shredded
        Harvarti or Swiss cheese
    1 cup (4 ounces) shredded
        Monterey Jack cheese
        Red Delicious apple slices
        tossed with lemon juice
        (optional)

Melt butter in medium saucepan over medium heat. Add onion; cook until softened, stirring occasionally. Stir in flour; cook until bubbly, stirring constantly. Gradually stir in chicken broth; cook until thickened, stirring constantly. Stir in applesauce; slowly stir in beer. Season with nutmeg, pepper, Worcestershire sauce and salt to taste. Reduce heat to low; simmer 10 to 15 minutes, stirring occasionally. Add ½ of the cheese; stir until melted. Add remaining cheese; stir until melted. Do not boil. Garnish each serving with apple slices. Makes 4 servings.

Frittata

    ¼ cup olive oil
    5 small onions, thinly sliced
    1 can (14½ ounces) tomatoes,
        drained, chopped
    ¼ pound cooked ham, chopped
    ¼ cup grated Parmesan cheese
    2 tablespoons minced parsley
    ½ teaspoon dried marjoram,
        crushed
    ¼ teaspoon dried basil, crushed
    ¼ teaspoon salt
        Dash pepper
    6 large eggs
    2 tablespoons butter

Heat oil in medium skillet over medium-high heat. Add onions; cook until onions are golden brown, 6 to 8 minutes, stirring frequently. Stir tomatoes into onions. Cook over medium heat 5 minutes, stirring constantly. With slotted spoon, transfer tomato mixture to large bowl; discard drippings. Let tomato mixture cool to room temperature.

Stir ham, cheese, parsley, marjoram, basil, salt and pepper into tomato mixture. Whisk eggs in small bowl; stir into ham mixture. Heat broiler. Heat butter in 10-inch heavy skillet with flameproof handle over medium heat. When foam subsides, reduce heat to very low. Add egg mixture to skillet; spread in even layer. Cook without stirring until all but top ¼ inch of the egg mixture is set, 8 to 10 minutes. Shake skillet gently to test. Place skillet in broiler. Broil frittata, 4 inches from heat, until top of egg mixture is set, 1 to 2 minutes. Do not let top brown or frittata will be dry. Frittata can be served hot, at room temperature or cold. Makes 6 to 8 appetizer servings.

Chicken and Tarragon Pastries

1½ cups chicken broth
9 ounces skinless, boneless chicken breast halves (3 halves)
¼ cup butter or margarine, divided
12 ounces mushrooms, sliced
1 small onion, chopped
3 tablespoons all-purpose flour
1 rib celery, chopped, or ½ cup chopped red bell pepper
1 teaspoon dried tarragon, crushed
Salt
Pepper
1 package (17¼ ounces) frozen puff pastry, thawed

Bring broth to a boil in medium saucepan over medium heat. Add chicken; reduce heat to low and poach 5 minutes. Remove from heat; let cool in broth.

Melt 2 tablespoons of the butter in large skillet over medium-high heat. Add mushrooms; cook 10 minutes or until lightly browned and juices evaporate, stirring occasionally. Remove from skillet and refrigerate. Remove chicken from broth; reserve broth. Coarsely chop chicken; set aside.

Melt remaining 2 tablespoons butter in medium saucepan over medium heat. Add onion; cook until softened, stirring occasionally. Stir in flour; cook until bubbly, stirring constantly. Gradually stir in ¾ cup of the reserved chicken broth; cook until thickened, stirring constantly. Stir in chicken, celery and tarragon. Season to taste with salt and pepper. Place in medium bowl. Refrigerate, covered, while preparing dough.

Unfold 1 pastry sheet onto lightly floured surface. Roll out pastry to 14×12-inch rectangle. Cut crosswise into 2 equal pieces. Spread ½ of the chicken mixture over 1 pastry half, leaving 1- to 1½-inch edges on all sides. Arrange ½ of the mushrooms over chicken. Brush edges with water. Place remaining piece of pastry over filling and seal edges. Flute if desired. Place on large cookie sheet. Refrigerate while repeating with remaining pastry and filling. Bake in preheated 425°F oven 25 minutes or until puffed and browned. Slide baked pastries onto platter. Cut into 2-inch slices. Makes about 10 appetizer servings.

Marinated Vegetable Medley

1 medium bunch broccoli, cut into flowerets (about 1 pound)
1 medium head cauliflower, cut into flowerets (about 1 pound)
1 small red onion, sliced, separated into rings
1 large green bell pepper, cut into strips
1 cup CRISCO® Oil
⅔ cup dry white wine
1 tablespoon Dijon-style mustard
½ to 1 teaspoon dried dill weed, crushed
1 teaspoon salt
1 teaspoon sugar
⅛ teaspoon pepper

Combine broccoli, cauliflower, onion and green pepper in large plastic bag. Combine remaining ingredients in medium bowl. Pour over vegetables; toss to coat. Tie bag. Marinate in refrigerator 1 or 2 days, turning bag over occasionally. Remove vegetables with slotted spoon before serving. Makes 8 to 10 appetizer servings.

Southwestern Scallops

1 pound bay scallops or 1 pound
    sea scallops, cut into quarters
½ cup lime juice
⅓ cup olive oil
1 teaspoon grated lime peel
1 green onion with top, sliced
    diagonally into ½-inch pieces
2 tablespoons chopped cilantro
1 tablespoon chopped parsley
  Salt
  Black pepper
½ cup Italian-style roasted
    peppers, cut into thin strips
1 avocado
  Lime juice
1 medium tomato, coarsely
    chopped
1 medium tomato, thinly sliced,
    cut into halves

Bring 3 inches salted water in large
saucepan over high heat to a boil.
Reduce heat to low. Add scallops;
poach 1 minute. Immediately drain
and rinse with cold water. Whisk the
½ cup lime juice, the oil and peel in
medium bowl until combined. Stir in
scallops, onion, cilantro and parsley.
Season to taste with salt and black
pepper. Stir in roasted peppers.
Refrigerate, covered, 1 hour or until
chilled. To serve, slice avocado; toss
with lime juice. Add avocado and
chopped tomato to scallop mixture.
Spoon into serving bowl. Arrange
tomato slices around edge of bowl.
Makes 6 appetizer servings.

Persian Spinach Salad

1½ tablespoons butter or margarine
3 tablespoons finely chopped
    onion
3 to 4 cups loosely packed,
    coarsely chopped fresh
    spinach leaves
2 cloves garlic, minced
1 cup (8 ounces) unflavored
    yogurt
  Salt
  Pepper
1 tablespoon chopped fresh mint
3 tablespoons chopped toasted
    walnuts

Melt butter in large skillet over
medium heat. Add onion; cook and
stir until onion is transparent. Add
spinach and garlic. Cook and toss just
until spinach is wilted. Remove from
heat. Drain thoroughly if needed.
Cool slightly, then combine spinach
mixture with yogurt. Season to taste
with salt and pepper. Serve at room
temperature, spooned onto individual
plates. Garnish with mint and
walnuts. Makes 4 to 6 appetizer
servings.

Favorite recipe from **Walnut Marketing
Board**

Southwestern Scallops

Pumpkin, Potato and Leek Soup

2 cups half and half
1 can (10¾ ounces) condensed cream of potato soup
1 cup LIBBY'S® Solid Pack Pumpkin
½ cup chopped leeks
¼ teaspoon salt
⅛ teaspoon pepper
⅛ teaspoon ground nutmeg

Combine half and half and soup in medium saucepan. Stir in remaining ingredients. Bring to a boil over medium heat, stirring frequently. Reduce heat to low. Simmer, covered, 5 minutes. Garnish as desired. Makes 4 cups, 4 to 6 servings.

Pumpkin, Potato and Leek Soup

Fettuccine with Goat Cheese, Swiss Chard and Walnuts

¼ cup olive oil
10 cups trimmed, lightly packed Swiss chard leaves, cut into narrow strips
3 cups whipping cream
1 cup goat cheese
½ cup coarsely chopped, toasted walnuts, divided
Pepper
12 ounces fettuccine, hot cooked, drained

Heat oil in large skillet over medium heat. Add Swiss chard and wilt quickly. Add cream, cheese and ¼ cup of the walnuts; cook and toss just until cheese melts. Season to taste with pepper. Add fettuccine; stir gently just to coat. Spoon onto 6 plates. Sprinkle with remaining ¼ cup walnuts. Makes 6 appetizer servings.

Favorite recipe from **Walnut Marketing Board**

Crab and Cheese Soufflé

    3 tablespoons butter or margarine
    3 tablespoons all-purpose flour
    ¾ cup milk
    ¼ cup half and half
    ⅛ teaspoon white pepper
    ½ teaspoon salt
    ½ teaspoon Dijon-style mustard
    ¼ teaspoon prepared horseradish
    4 large eggs, separated
    ½ cup (2 ounces) shredded Swiss
        cheese
    6 ounces crabmeat, picked over
    ⅛ teaspoon cream of tartar

Grease 4 (3½- to 4-inch) soufflé dishes (about 1 cup each). Melt butter in medium saucepan over medium heat. Stir in flour; cook until bubbly, stirring constantly. Gradually stir in milk and half and half; cook until thickened, stirring constantly. Stir in pepper, salt, mustard and horseradish. Remove from heat. Beat in egg yolks, one at a time. Stir in cheese until melted. Stir in crabmeat. Beat egg whites with cream of tartar in large bowl until stiff peaks form. Stir ¼ of the egg whites into cheese mixture to lighten. Fold in remaining egg whites. Divide mixture among dishes. Bake in preheated 375°F oven 25 to 30 minutes or until puffed and lightly browned on top. Serve immediately. Makes 4 appetizer servings.

Ham-Stuffed Artichoke Hearts

    2 cans (13¾ ounces each)
        artichoke hearts, drained,
        rinsed
    2 ounces finely chopped ham
    ½ cup (2 ounces) shredded Swiss
        cheese
    2 tablespoons seasoned dry
        bread crumbs
    ½ teaspoon dried oregano,
        crushed
    Pepper
    Dry white wine

Grease 8×8-inch baking pan. Carefully open each artichoke heart with your fingers to expose the choke. With spoon, remove choke; do not cut through bottom of heart. Discard chokes. Cut off pointed tips on bottoms of artichoke hearts so they will sit flat. Combine ham, cheese, bread crumbs, oregano, pepper to taste and about 1 tablespoon wine in medium bowl. Mixture should be slightly moist. Stuff about 1 tablespoon of the mixture into each artichoke heart. Arrange in pan. Bake in preheated 425°F oven 15 minutes or until hot and cheese melts. Makes about 12 to 14 appetizer servings.

PUTTING ON THE RITZ

Oyster-Stuffed Tomatoes

30 cherry tomatoes
1 can (3¾ ounces) smoked oysters, drained
4 ounces cream cheese, softened
1½ teaspoons lemon juice
1½ teaspoons prepared horseradish
Dash hot pepper sauce
Dill or parsley sprigs

Cut slit in blossom end of each tomato large enough to insert an oyster. Invert on paper towels and let drain. Insert 1 oyster, lengthwise, in each tomato. Arrange on serving plate. Beat cream cheese, lemon juice, horseradish and hot pepper sauce in small bowl until light and fluffy. Pipe cream cheese mixture, using a star tip, on 1 side of each oyster. Garnish with dill sprig. Makes 30 appetizers.

Mandarin Plum Chicken Bites

- **1 can (20 ounces) DOLE® Chunk Pineapple in Syrup**
- **2 whole skinless, boneless chicken breasts**
- **1 cup plum jam, melted**
- **3 tablespoons soy sauce**
- **1 tablespoon dry sherry**
- **¼ teaspoon garlic powder**
- **¼ teaspoon ground ginger**
- **1 teaspoon cornstarch**
- **1 large red or green bell pepper**

Soak 40 (8-inch) bamboo skewers in water 30 minutes. (Other thin, broiler-proof skewers may be used.)

Drain pineapple. Cut chicken into 40 bite-sized pieces; place in plastic bag. Combine jam, soy sauce, sherry, garlic powder and ginger in small bowl; pour over chicken, turning to coat. Tie bag. Marinate in refrigerator 2 hours. Drain sauce into small saucepan. Stir in cornstarch. Heat over medium-high heat until sauce boils and thickens, stirring constantly. Cut pepper into 40 pieces. Arrange chicken, pineapple and pepper on skewers. Arrange on broiler pan. Baste chicken with sauce. Broil, 4 inches from heat, about 10 minutes, turning and basting once. Baste again before serving. Makes 40 appetizers.

Appetizer Ham Logs

2 cups ground ham
1 egg, beaten
¼ teaspoon pepper
¼ cup seasoned fine dry bread
crumbs
½ cup horseradish sauce
1 tablespoon prepared mustard
⅛ teaspoon celery salt
Vegetable oil for frying
Pimiento strips

Combine ham, egg and pepper in medium bowl; mix well. Shape into 1-inch logs or balls. Roll in bread crumbs. Refrigerate, covered, 1 hour.

To make mustard sauce, combine horseradish sauce, mustard and celery salt in small bowl until well blended. Refrigerate, covered, until serving time.

Heat 3 inches oil in heavy, large saucepan over medium-high heat until oil is 365°F; adjust heat to maintain temperature. Fry ham logs, a few at a time, 2 to 3 minutes or until golden. Drain on paper towels. Garnish with pimiento strips. Serve with mustard sauce. Makes about 24 appetizers.

Favorite recipe from **National Pork Producers Council**

Rumaki

16 slices bacon
1 pound chicken livers, cut into
quarters
1 can (8 ounces) sliced water
chestnuts, drained
⅓ cup soy sauce
2 tablespoons packed brown
sugar
1 tablespoon Dijon-style mustard

Cut bacon slices in half crosswise. Wrap ½ slice bacon around piece of chicken liver and water chestnut slice. Secure with wooden pick. (Reserve any remaining water chestnut slices for another use.) Arrange on broiler pan. Combine soy sauce, brown sugar and mustard in small bowl. Brush over bacon rolls. Broil, 6 inches from heat, 15 to 20 minutes or until bacon is crisp and chicken livers are done, turning and brushing with soy sauce mixture occasionally. Makes about 32 appetizers.

Favorite recipe from **National Pork Producers Council**

Ham-Wrapped Oysters

3 tablespoons prepared
horseradish
½ pound ham, cut into
3×1×¼-inch strips
2 dozen fresh oysters, shucked
3 tablespoons butter or
margarine, melted
1 tablespoon lemon juice
¼ teaspoon garlic powder

Spread horseradish on 1 side of each ham strip. Place 1 oyster on each ham strip; roll up and secure with wooden pick. Arrange on broiler pan. Combine butter, lemon juice and garlic powder in small cup. Brush each ham roll with some of the lemon-butter. Broil, 5 inches from heat, 10 to 15 minutes or until edges of oysters curl, brushing occasionally with the remaining lemon-butter. Makes 24 appetizers.

Favorite recipe from **National Pork Producers Council**

Top: Appetizer Ham Logs, Miniature Teriyaki Pork Kabobs (page 18); bottom: Ham-Wrapped Oysters, Rumaki

Miniature Teriyaki Pork Kabobs

**1 pound boneless pork, cut into
4×1×½-inch strips**
**1 can (11 ounces) mandarin
oranges**
**1 small green bell pepper, cut into
1×¼×¼-inch strips**
¼ cup teriyaki sauce
1 tablespoon honey
1 tablespoon vinegar
⅛ teaspoon garlic powder

Soak 24 (8-inch) bamboo skewers in
water 10 minutes. Thread pork strips
accordion-style with mandarin
oranges on skewers. Place 1 pepper
strip on end of each skewer. Arrange
on broiler pan.

For sauce, combine teriyaki sauce,
honey, vinegar and garlic powder in
small bowl; mix well. Brush sauce
over kabobs. Broil, 6 inches from
heat, about 15 minutes or until pork
is done, turning and basting with
sauce occasionally. Makes about 24
appetizers.

Favorite recipe from **National Pork
Producers Council**

Simply Delicious Salmon Spread

**2 envelopes KNOX® Unflavored
Gelatine**
½ cup cold water
1 cup boiling water
2 cups dairy sour cream
**¾ cup WISH-BONE® Thousand
Island Dressing**
1 tablespoon lemon juice
**1 can (15½ ounces) salmon,
drained, flaked**
½ cup chopped onion
1 teaspoon dried dill weed

Sprinkle unflavored gelatine over cold
water in large bowl; let stand 1
minute. Add boiling water and stir
until gelatine is completely dissolved.
Whisk in sour cream, Thousand
Island dressing and lemon juice. Stir
in salmon, onion and dill weed. Pour
into 5½-cup mold or bowl; refrigerate
until firm. Makes 5½ cups.

Beef Fondue

Mustard Sauce (recipe follows)
Oriental Sauce (recipe follows)
1 clove garlic, cut into halves
CRISCO® Oil for frying
**1 to 1½ pounds boneless beef
sirloin, cut into ¾-inch cubes**

Prepare Mustard Sauce and Oriental
Sauce. Rub inside of fondue pot with
cut sides of garlic. Discard garlic.
Heat 2 inches oil in fondue pot to
375°F. Place pot over flame to keep
warm.

Place beef cubes on fondue forks. Fry
beef in hot oil about 1 minute for
medium-rare doneness. Dip beef in
sauces. Makes 8 to 10 servings.

Mustard Sauce: Blend 2 tablespoons
CRISCO® Oil, 2 tablespoons all-
purpose flour, 2 tablespoons dry
mustard and ½ teaspoon salt in small
saucepan. Cook over medium-high
heat 1 minute. Stir in 1 cup milk.
Cook, stirring constantly, until sauce
thickens and bubbles. Makes about 1
cup. Refrigerate, covered, until ready
to use.

Oriental Sauce: Blend ¼ cup soy
sauce, ¼ cup water, 1 teaspoon sugar
and 1 teaspoon ground ginger in small
bowl. Sprinkle with finely chopped
green onion. Makes about ½ cup.

Caramelized Onion, Walnut and Gorgonzola Pizza

Basic Pizza Dough (recipe follows)
¼ **cup unsalted butter**
10 **cups thinly sliced red onions (about 10 medium)**
Salt
Pepper
1 **cup crumbled Gorgonzola cheese**
1 **cup toasted walnut pieces**
Olive oil

Prepare Basic Pizza Dough. Melt butter in large, heavy skillet over low heat. Add onions and cook slowly, stirring occasionally, about 30 minutes until onions are soft and golden. Season to taste with salt and pepper. Spread onion mixture evenly on prepared, uncooked pizza dough rounds. Sprinkle Gorgonzola over onions. Sprinkle with walnuts. Bake in preheated 450°F oven until crust is puffed and golden, about 12 minutes. Lightly brush edge of crust with olive oil. Makes 4 (6-inch) or 2 (12-inch) pizzas.

Basic Pizza Dough: Dissolve 1 envelope (¼ ounce) active dry yeast in ¼ cup warm water (110° to 115°F) in large bowl. Add ½ cup unbleached flour; mix to combine. Let sit in warm place, covered, 30 minutes.

Add 1¾ cups unbleached flour, ⅓ cup rye flour, ¾ cup water, 3 tablespoons olive oil and 1½ teaspoons salt to dough mixture. Mix to blend. Knead dough (dough will be soft and sticky) on lightly floured surface 10 to 15 minutes. Transfer dough to greased bowl, cover with plastic wrap and allow to rise in warm place until doubled, about 1 hour. Punch down dough on lightly floured surface. Shape into 2 equal balls; cover and allow to rest in refrigerator 30 minutes. Stretch into rounds on baking sheets. Makes 4 (6-inch) or 2 (12-inch) pizzas.

Favorite recipe from **Walnut Marketing Board**

Chicken Wing Drumsticks

12 **chicken wings**
⅓ **cup sesame seeds**
⅔ **cup fine dry bread crumbs**
½ **teaspoon paprika**
½ **teaspoon salt**
½ **teaspoon seasoned salt**
½ **cup half and half**
¼ **cup butter or margarine, melted**

Remove and discard wing tips. Separate remaining wing sections. Cut skin at small end of each wing section. Pull out one of the bones from section having 2 bones; set aside.

Toast sesame seeds in small skillet over low heat until golden, stirring occasionally. Combine toasted sesame seeds, bread crumbs, paprika, salt and seasoned salt in small, shallow dish. Pour half and half into another shallow dish. Dip wing sections into half and half, then into bread crumb mixture. Arrange in 13×9-inch baking pan. Pour melted butter over chicken. Bake at 350°F 45 to 55 minutes until chicken is done. Makes 24 appetizers.

Miniature Egg Rolls

2 cups thinly sliced napa cabbage
1 teaspoon vegetable oil
½ pound sliced honey loaf, cut into thin strips
4 green onions with tops, cut into thin slices
¾ cup unsweetened pineapple juice
¼ cup packed brown sugar
¼ cup cider vinegar
3 tablespoons cornstarch, divided
1 teaspoon soy sauce
2 tablespoons water
32 wonton wrappers
Vegetable oil for frying
Sweet and sour sauce for dipping

Cook and stir cabbage in oil in medium nonstick skillet over medium heat 3 to 5 minutes. Remove from heat; stir in honey loaf and onions; set aside. Combine pineapple juice, brown sugar, vinegar, 1 tablespoon of the cornstarch and the soy sauce in small saucepan. Cook over high heat 2 minutes, stirring occasionally. Cover sauce; set aside.

Mix remaining 2 tablespoons cornstarch and the water in cup until smooth. Just before filling, brush cornstarch mixture lightly over 1 side of wonton wrapper. Place 1 tablespoon of the honey loaf mixture in center of each wonton wrapper. Fold 1 corner over filling, then bring 2 adjacent corners together; fold remaining corner over to enclose filling.

Heat 3 inches oil in heavy, large saucepan over medium-high heat until oil is 375°F; adjust heat to maintain temperature. Fry egg rolls, 4 to 6 at a time, 2 minutes or until golden brown, turning once. Drain on paper towels. Serve with sweet and sour sauce. Makes 32 egg rolls.

Favorite recipe from **National Live Stock and Meat Board**

Antipasto Beef Kabobs

2 pounds beef top round steak, cut ¾ to 1 inch thick
⅔ cup lemon juice
⅓ cup vegetable oil
1 tablespoon Worcestershire sauce
1 tablespoon instant minced onion
2 teaspoons sugar
2 teaspoons dried oregano, crushed
1 teaspoon dried basil, crushed
1 teaspoon garlic salt
½ teaspoon pepper
Stuffed green olives

Partially freeze steak and slice into ⅛-inch thick strips. Combine lemon juice, oil, Worcestershire sauce, instant minced onion, sugar, oregano, basil, garlic salt and pepper in small saucepan. Bring to a boil over high heat. Reduce heat to low; simmer 10 minutes, stirring occasionally. Cool.

Place meat in plastic bag; add marinade, turning to coat. Tie bag. Marinate in refrigerator at least 4 hours.

Soak about 15 (8-inch) bamboo skewers in water 10 minutes. Remove steak strips from marinade. Thread 2 strips on each skewer by weaving back and forth. Place 1 olive on end of each skewer. Arrange kabobs in jelly-roll pan. Bake in preheated 450°F oven 5 to 8 minutes for rare to medium doneness. Serve with assorted peppers and cheeses if desired. Makes about 15 appetizers.

Favorite recipe from **National Live Stock and Meat Board**

Green Onion Canapés

**1 package (8 ounces) cream
    cheese, softened
½ cup chopped green onions
¼ cup HELLMANN'S® or BEST
    FOODS® Real Mayonnaise
Assorted crackers
Sliced ripe olives
Red caviar**

Beat cream cheese in small bowl until
light and fluffy. Beat in onions and
mayonnaise until well blended.
Refrigerate, covered, at least 4 hours
to blend flavors. Pipe or spread on
crackers. Garnish with ripe olive
slices or red caviar. Makes 1¾ cups.

Deviled Eggs

**6 hard-cooked eggs, cut into
    halves
¼ cup HELLMANN'S® or BEST
    FOODS® Real Mayonnaise
1 teaspoon prepared mustard
½ teaspoon white vinegar
¼ teaspoon salt
Paprika**

Remove egg yolks from whites; place
in small bowl. Mash yolks with fork.
Stir in mayonnaise, mustard, vinegar
and salt. Spoon or pipe yolk mixture
into hollows of egg whites.
Refrigerate, covered, 1 hour. Sprinkle
with paprika. Makes 12 appetizers.

Variation: Add one of these for a
different taste: 2 tablespoons
crumbled cooked bacon; or 1
tablespoon chopped green onion, ¾
teaspoon chili powder and hot pepper
sauce to taste.

Stuffed French Bread

**1 loaf French bread (about
    20 inches long)
2 packages (8 ounces each)
    cream cheese, softened
½ cup HELLMANN'S® or BEST
    FOODS® Real Mayonnaise
1 jar (4 ounces) diced pimientos,
    well drained
¼ cup chopped parsley
½ teaspoon seasoned salt
⅛ teaspoon garlic powder**

Cut bread crosswise into quarters.
With fork, hollow out center of each
quarter, leaving ½-inch shell; set
aside. Beat remaining ingredients in
medium bowl until well blended. Pack
mixture into bread. Wrap in plastic
wrap; refrigerate at least 3 hours. Just
before serving, cut into ½-inch slices.
Makes about 40 appetizers.

Crab-Stuffed Cherry Tomatoes

**1 pint cherry tomatoes
1 package (6 ounces) frozen
    crabmeat, thawed, well
    drained, picked over
¼ cup HELLMANN'S® or BEST
    FOODS® Real Mayonnaise
¾ teaspoon grated lemon peel
½ teaspoon curry powder
¼ teaspoon salt**

Cut a thin slice off tops and bottoms
of tomatoes. Remove pulp from stem
end; drain on paper towels. Combine
remaining ingredients in small bowl
until well blended. Fill tomatoes.
Refrigerate, covered, until ready to
serve. Makes about 20 appetizers.

*Assortment includes: Green Onion
Canapés, Deviled Eggs, Stuffed
French Bread, Crab-Stuffed Cherry
Tomatoes and Tuna-Stuffed
Mushrooms (page 24)*

Tuna-Stuffed Mushrooms

12 large mushrooms
1 can (3½ ounces) tuna, drained, flaked
½ cup HELLMANN'S® or BEST FOODS® Real Mayonnaise
3 tablespoons grated Parmesan cheese
3 tablespoons fine dry bread crumbs
1 teaspoon minced onion
1 teaspoon lemon juice

Remove and finely chop mushroom stems. Combine chopped stems and remaining ingredients in medium bowl until well blended. Arrange mushroom caps, rounded side up, on broiler pan. Broil, 4 inches from heat, 5 minutes. Turn caps over; fill with tuna mixture. Broil 5 minutes more or until lightly browned. Garnish as desired. Makes 12 appetizers.

Microwave Directions: Prepare filling as directed. Fill mushroom caps with tuna mixture. Arrange in circle on microwave-safe plate. Microwave at High 2 to 3 minutes, rotating plate ½ turn after each minute.

Shrimp Tempura

Oriental Sauce (see page 18)
1 cup all-purpose flour
½ teaspoon salt
1 cup ice water
1 egg, slightly beaten
2 tablespoons CRISCO® Oil
CRISCO® Oil for frying
1 pound medium shrimp, peeled, deveined and butterflied, with tails attached

Prepare Oriental Sauce. Combine flour and salt in small bowl. Add water, egg and the 2 tablespoons oil. Stir until smooth. Refrigerate covered.

Heat 3 inches oil in heavy, large saucepan over medium-high heat until oil is 375°F; adjust heat to maintain temperature. Dip shrimp, a few at a time, in batter. Fry 2 to 3 minutes or until light golden brown, turning over once. Drain on paper towels. Serve immediately or keep warm in 175°F oven. Serve with Oriental Sauce. Makes 6 to 8 servings.

Vegetable Tempura: Follow above recipe, substituting 4 cups fresh parsley sprigs, 4 medium green bell peppers (cut into ½-inch strips) or 1 pound carrots (cut into julienne strips) for the shrimp.

Tangy Blue Cheese Whip

1 cup whipping cream
½ cup (2 ounces) finely crumbled Wisconsin blue cheese
1 teaspoon dried basil, crushed
¼ teaspoon garlic salt
½ cup almonds, toasted, chopped
Assorted vegetables or fruit for dippers

Combine whipping cream, blue cheese, basil and garlic salt in small bowl. Beat until slightly thickened. Gently fold in chopped almonds. Refrigerate, covered, up to 2 hours if desired. Serve with assorted vegetables or fruit. Makes about 2 cups.

Favorite recipe from **Wisconsin Milk Marketing Board**©

Cheesy Deep-Fried Broccoli

     4 cups water
     ¾ teaspoon salt, divided
     3 cups fresh broccoli flowerets
     ¾ cup all-purpose flour, divided
     4 tablespoons grated American
        cheese food, divided
     ¼ teaspoon onion powder
     1 cup buttermilk
     ½ teaspoon baking powder
        CRISCO® Oil for frying

Combine water and ½ teaspoon of the salt in large saucepan. Bring to a boil over high heat. Add broccoli; return to a boil. Boil 3 minutes; drain and rinse under cold water. Mix ¼ cup of the flour, 2 tablespoons of the cheese and the onion powder in large plastic bag. Add broccoli; shake to coat. Set aside.

Combine buttermilk, baking powder, remaining ½ cup flour, 2 tablespoons cheese and ¼ teaspoon salt in small bowl. Stir until smooth.

Heat 3 inches oil in heavy, large saucepan over medium-high heat until oil is 375°F; adjust heat to maintain temperature. Dip broccoli, a few pieces at a time, in batter. Let excess batter drip back into bowl. Fry 1 to 2 minutes or until deep golden brown. Drain on paper towels. Serve immediately or keep warm in 175°F oven. Makes 10 to 12 servings.

Baked Artichoke Squares

     ½ cup plus 3 tablespoons
        CRISCO® Oil, divided
     1 cup chopped mushrooms
     ¼ cup thinly sliced celery
     1 clove garlic, minced
     1 can (13¾ ounces) artichoke
        hearts, drained, chopped
     ⅓ cup chopped green onions
     ½ teaspoon dried marjoram,
        crushed
     ¼ teaspoon dried oregano,
        crushed
     ¼ teaspoon ground red pepper
     1 cup (4 ounces) shredded
        Cheddar cheese
     1 cup (4 ounces) shredded
        Monterey Jack cheese
     2 eggs, slightly beaten
     1½ cups all-purpose flour
     ½ teaspoon salt
     ¼ cup milk

Heat 3 tablespoons of the oil in medium skillet over medium-high heat. Cook and stir mushrooms, celery and garlic in hot oil until celery is tender. Remove from heat. Stir in artichoke hearts, onions, marjoram, oregano and ground red pepper. Add cheeses and eggs; mix well. Set aside.

Combine flour and salt in medium bowl. Blend remaining ½ cup oil and the milk in small bowl. Add to flour mixture. Stir with fork until mixture forms a ball. Press dough in bottom and 1½ inches up sides of 13×9×2-inch pan. Bake in preheated 350°F oven 10 minutes. Spread artichoke mixture on baked crust. Continue baking about 20 minutes more or until center is set. Cool slightly. Cut into 24 squares. Serve warm. Makes 24 appetizers.

Wisconsin Brie Torte

    1 wheel (14 ounces) or 2 wheels
        (8 ounces each) ripe
        Wisconsin Brie cheese
  ½ cup butter, softened
    1 large clove garlic, pressed
  ⅓ cup finely chopped walnuts
  ⅓ cup finely chopped ripe olives
    2 tablespoons chopped basil
        leaves or 2 teaspoons dried
        basil, crushed
        Assorted crackers

Place Brie in freezer about ½ hour until very firm. Carefully cut into halves, horizontally; set aside. Cream butter and garlic in small bowl. Mix in walnuts, olives and basil until blended. Spread evenly on cut side of 1 of the Brie halves. Top with the other half, cut side down. Press together lightly. Wrap in plastic wrap and refrigerate until chilled. Bring to room temperature before serving. Serve with assorted crackers. Makes 12 appetizers.

Favorite recipe from **Wisconsin Milk Marketing Board**©

Salmon Puff Appetizers

    1 can (15½ ounces) pink salmon
    3 egg yolks, at room temperature
  1½ teaspoons lemon juice
    1 tablespoon hot water
  ¾ cup butter or margarine, melted
  ¾ teaspoon prepared mustard
    1 tablespoon chopped parsley
    1 tablespoon chopped chives
    3 sheets frozen puff pastry,
        thawed
    1 egg, beaten

Drain salmon; remove skin and bones if desired. Place salmon in small bowl; break into small chunks with fork.

Beat egg yolks and lemon juice in blender. Blend in hot water. At high speed, add hot melted butter in slow, steady stream. Add mustard and blend 30 seconds longer. Pour into bowl. Fold in parsley and chives. Let cool slightly. Fold in salmon. Refrigerate covered.

Roll out each sheet on lightly floured surface into 18×12-inch rectangle. Cut each sheet into 24 (3-inch) squares. Place small spoonful of the salmon mixture in one corner of each square. Brush edges of pastry with beaten egg; fold over to form small triangle. Seal by pressing edges with fork. Freeze until needed.

To serve, arrange on cookie sheet. Brush tops lightly with beaten egg. Bake in preheated 350°F oven 25 to 30 minutes or until puffed and golden. Makes 72 appetizers.

Curried Chicken Spread

    2 cups finely chopped cooked
        chicken
    2 green onions with tops, finely
        chopped
    3 tablespoons chopped almonds
  ¼ cup mayonnaise
    1 tablespoon mango chutney
    1 teaspoon lemon juice
    1 teaspoon curry powder
  ¼ teaspoon salt
        Assorted crackers

Combine all ingredients except crackers in medium bowl until well blended. Refrigerate, covered, until ready to serve. Serve with assorted crackers. Makes about 2 cups.

Wisconsin Brie Torte

Cheesy Pumpkin-Ham Soufflés

Grated Parmesan cheese
¼ cup butter or margarine
1 cup LIBBY'S® Solid Pack
   Pumpkin
¼ cup all-purpose flour
1 tablespoon prepared mustard
1 cup milk
6 large eggs, separated
1 cup finely chopped ham
1 cup (4 ounces) shredded Swiss
   cheese
¼ cup grated Parmesan cheese

Butter bottom and sides of 5 to 6 (10-ounce) custard cups or soufflé dishes; dust lightly with Parmesan cheese. Melt butter in medium saucepan over medium-high heat. Add pumpkin, flour and mustard; mix well. Slowly stir in milk. Cook until mixture comes to a boil, stirring constantly. Stir ¼ cup of the pumpkin mixture into the egg yolks. Stir egg mixture back into saucepan; cook over low heat 2 minutes, stirring constantly. Remove from heat; stir in ham and cheeses. Beat egg whites in narrow bowl until stiff peaks form. Fold into pumpkin mixture. Pour into prepared dishes. Bake in preheated 375°F oven 25 minutes or until tops are golden brown. Makes 5 to 6 servings.

Middle Eastern Meatballs

1 pound lean ground beef
1 egg, slightly beaten
3 tablespoons minced onion
1 clove garlic, minced
1 tablespoon cornstarch
½ teaspoon salt
   Dash Worcestershire sauce
1 can (8 ounces) tomato sauce
½ cup apple juice
¼ cup catsup
¼ cup honey
¾ teaspoon dry mustard
⅛ teaspoon ground cinnamon

Combine beef, egg, onion, garlic, cornstarch, salt and Worcestershire sauce in medium bowl. Shape into meatballs using 1 tablespoonful of mixture for each. Arrange in jelly-roll pan. Bake in preheated 475°F oven 10 to 15 minutes or until browned.

Meanwhile, prepare sauce. Combine tomato sauce, apple juice, catsup, honey, mustard and cinnamon in medium saucepan. Cook over medium heat 10 minutes, stirring occasionally. Add browned meatballs. Reduce heat to low; cook 5 minutes more. Spoon into chafing dish. Makes about 32 meatballs.

Tapenade Dip

    1 can (6½ ounces) solid white
        tuna, drained
    4 anchovy fillets
    1 large clove garlic
    ½ cup pitted ripe olives
    ½ cup parsley
    ½ cup fresh basil leaves or
        2 teaspoons dried basil,
        crushed
    ¼ cup pitted green olives
    ¼ cup olive oil
    ¼ cup mayonnaise
        Assorted vegetables for dippers

Combine tuna, anchovy fillets, garlic, ripe olives, parsley, basil and green olives in blender or food processor. Cover and process until smooth. With motor still running, very slowly pour oil into feed tube to make a smooth, thick sauce. Stir in mayonnaise. Serve with assorted vegetables. Makes about 1½ cups.

Oriental Chicken Strips

        Oriental Sauce (see page 18)
    ¼ cup all-purpose flour
    2 tablespoons cornstarch
    ½ teaspoon ground ginger
    ¼ cup water
    1 egg
    1 tablespoon soy sauce
    ¼ teaspoon sesame oil
    2 slices bacon, cooked, finely
        crumbled
    1 tablespoon minced green onion
    2 large whole skinless, boneless
        chicken breasts, cut into
        4×½-inch strips
        CRISCO® Oil for frying

Prepare Oriental Sauce. Combine flour, cornstarch and ginger in medium bowl. Blend in water, egg, soy sauce and sesame oil. Stir in bacon and onion. Add chicken strips. Stir to coat.

Heat ¼ inch oil in heavy, medium skillet over medium-high heat. Fry chicken strips, a few at a time, 4 to 5 minutes or until golden brown, turning over once.* Add additional oil to skillet as needed. Drain on paper towels. Serve immediately or keep warm in 175°F oven. Serve with Oriental Sauce. Makes 6 to 8 servings.

*To make 1 day ahead, prepare and fry as directed. Cool. Refrigerate covered. Reheat in single layer on ungreased baking sheet in preheated 400°F oven 5 to 8 minutes or until hot.

Cheesy Pumpkin-Ham Soufflé

Fried Cheese Wedges

1 pound Wisconsin Monterey
   Jack or Cheddar cheese (in
   brick form)
1 cup fine dry bread crumbs
1 cup toasted wheat germ
¼ teaspoon ground red pepper
1 tablespoon butter
1 can (8 ounces) tomato sauce
1 can (2 ounces) mushroom
   stems and pieces, drained,
   chopped
½ teaspoon dried basil, crushed
½ teaspoon dried oregano,
   crushed
4 eggs, beaten
   Vegetable oil for frying

Cut cheese into 2×1½×¾-inch
rectangles, then cut each rectangle
into 2 wedges. Refrigerate, covered,
until chilled. Combine bread crumbs,
wheat germ and ground red pepper in
shallow dish; set aside.

Melt butter in medium saucepan over
medium heat. Stir in tomato sauce,
mushrooms, basil and oregano. Bring
to a boil over high heat. Reduce heat
to low; simmer, uncovered, 5 minutes,
stirring occasionally. Cover and keep
warm while preparing cheese.

Dip chilled cheese wedges into beaten
eggs; coat evenly, then roll in bread
crumb mixture. Dip wedges into eggs
and roll in crumb mixture again.

Heat 3 inches oil in heavy 3-quart
saucepan over medium-high heat
until oil is 375°F; adjust heat to
maintain temperature. Fry cheese
wedges, a few at a time, 30 to 60
seconds or until golden brown on all
sides. Drain on paper towels. Keep
warm in 250°F oven while frying
remaining cheese. Serve warm with
sauce. Makes about 20 appetizers.

Favorite recipe from **Wisconsin Milk
Marketing Board**©

Mini Lamb Kabobs

⅓ cup vegetable oil
⅓ cup vinegar
2 cloves garlic, minced
2 teaspoons dried basil, crushed
1 teaspoon salt
⅛ teaspoon black pepper
1 pound boneless lamb, cut into
   3×¾×¼-inch strips
2 ribs celery, cut into 24 pieces
1 medium red bell pepper, cut into
   24 pieces

Combine oil, vinegar, garlic, basil, salt
and black pepper in small saucepan.
Bring to a boil over high heat. Reduce
heat to low; simmer 4 to 5 minutes.
Cool.

Place lamb in plastic bag; add ½ of
the marinade, turning to coat. Tie
bag. Place celery and red pepper in
another plastic bag; add remaining ½
marinade, turning to coat. Tie bag.
Marinate meat and vegetables in
refrigerator at least 6 hours, turning
at least once.

Soak 24 (8-inch) bamboo skewers in
water 10 minutes. Remove meat from
marinade; discard marinade. Thread
lamb strips on skewers by weaving
strips back and forth. Remove
vegetables from marinade; reserve
marinade. Place 1 celery piece and 1
red pepper piece on end of each
skewer. Arrange kabobs on broiler
pan. Broil, 3 to 4 inches from heat, 5
to 7 minutes, turning and basting
with reserved marinade occasionally.
Makes 24 mini-kabobs.

Favorite recipe from **National Live Stock and
Meat Board**

Spinach-Cheese Triangles

½ cup minced onion
2 tablespoons butter or margarine
1 package (10 ounces) frozen
    chopped spinach, thawed,
    squeezed dry
½ cup finely chopped parsley
2 tablespoons minced green
    onions
¼ pound feta cheese, crumbled
2 eggs, beaten
1 package (17¼ ounces) frozen
    puff pastry, thawed
1 egg beaten with 1 teaspoon
    water

Cook and stir onions in butter in large skillet over medium-high heat until onions are transparent; remove from heat. Add spinach, parsley, green onions, cheese and the 2 eggs, mixing thoroughly.

Unfold 1 pastry and roll out to 15×15-inch square on lightly floured surface. Cut into 25 (3-inch) squares. Repeat with remaining pastry. Place about 2 teaspoons of the spinach mixture in one corner of each square. Brush edges of pastry with egg-water mixture; fold pastry over to form triangle. Seal by pressing edges with fork. Brush tops with egg-water mixture. Bake in preheated 375°F oven 12 to 15 minutes. Makes 5C appetizers.

Favorite recipe from **National Live Stock and Meat Board**

Top: Spinach-Cheese Triangles; bottom: Mini Lamb Kabobs

EXTRA EASY

Nacho Rio Grande

½ cup butter or margarine
1 package (1¾ ounces) chili seasoning
1 tablespoon Worcestershire sauce
8 cups CORN CHEX® Brand Cereal
2 cups (8 ounces) shredded Cheddar cheese
2 tablespoons chopped green chilies

Melt butter in large, shallow roasting pan in preheated 350°F oven. Stir in chili seasoning and Worcestershire sauce. Gradually add cereal, stirring until all pieces are evenly coated. Bake 15 minutes, stirring every 5 minutes.* Top with cheese and chilies. Return to oven 5 to 10 minutes. Serve immediately. Makes 8 cups.

*To prepare ahead: After baking, cool mixture on paper towels, then store in airtight container until ready to serve. Place cereal on ovenproof platter. Top with cheese and chilies. Bake in preheated 350°F oven 10 minutes or until cheese melts. Serve immediately.

Cheese Crunchies

2½ cups CORN CHEX® Brand Cereal, crushed to make 1 cup
¾ teaspoon chili seasoning
½ cup plus 2 tablespoons butter or margarine, softened, divided
1¼ cups (5 ounces) shredded sharp Cheddar cheese
1 cup all-purpose flour
½ teaspoon onion powder
¼ teaspoon seasoned salt

Combine cereal crumbs and chili seasoning in small bowl. Melt 2 tablespoons of the butter in small saucepan over low heat. Stir into crumbs; set aside. Beat cheese and remaining ½ cup butter in medium bowl until smooth. Blend in flour, ½ cup of the seasoned crumbs, the onion powder and seasoned salt. Shape mixture into 1-inch balls. Roll in remaining seasoned crumbs. Place on ungreased baking sheet. Flatten to ¼ inch with bottom of glass. Bake in preheated 350°F oven 12 to 14 minutes or until golden. Best served the same day. Makes about 30 appetizers.

Clockwise from top center: Great Garlic Party Mix (page 34), Cheese Crunchies, Sweet'n Crunchy Fruit Mix (page 34), Nacho Rio Grande

Great Garlic Party Mix

⅓ cup vegetable oil
2 tablespoons red wine vinegar
1 package (¾ ounces) garlic and herb salad dressing mix
3 cups CORN CHEX® Brand Cereal
3 cups WHEAT CHEX® Brand Cereal
½ cup slivered almonds

Combine oil, vinegar and salad dressing mix in 13×9×2-inch baking pan. Gradually add cereals and nuts, stirring until all pieces are evenly coated. Bake in preheated 350°F oven 20 minutes. Stir halfway through baking time. Spread on paper towels to cool. Store in airtight container. Makes 6 cups.

Sweet 'n Crunchy Fruit Mix

6 tablespoons butter or margarine
½ cup unsweetened pineapple juice
¼ cup packed brown sugar
2 cups chopped dried fruit
3 cups CORN CHEX® Brand Cereal
3 cups RICE CHEX® Brand Cereal
3 cups WHEAT CHEX® Brand Cereal
½ cup flaked coconut
½ cup sunflower seeds

Melt butter in large skillet over medium heat. Add pineapple juice, sugar and fruit. Bring to a boil. Boil 2 minutes, stirring frequently. Gradually add cereals, coconut and sunflower seeds, stirring until all pieces are evenly coated. Cook 10 minutes, stirring frequently. Spread on waxed paper to cool. Store in airtight container. Makes 9 cups.

Microwave Directions: Microwave butter in 4-quart microwave-safe bowl at High 1 minute. Stir in pineapple juice, sugar and fruit. Microwave at High 2 minutes. Gradually add cereals, coconut and sunflower seeds, stirring until all pieces are evenly coated. Microwave at High 4½ to 5 minutes, stirring every 1½ minutes. Spread on waxed paper to cool. Store in airtight container. Makes 9 cups.

Fluffy Fruit Dip

⅓ cup apricot preserves or orange marmalade
1 cup dairy sour cream
¼ cup finely chopped walnuts
2 to 3 tablespoons milk
Assorted fruit for dippers
Assorted Wisconsin cheeses, cut up

Cut up any large pieces of fruit in the preserves; place in small bowl. Stir in sour cream and walnuts. Add enough milk to make mixture the consistency for dipping. Refrigerate, covered, at least 1 hour to blend flavors. Serve with assorted fruit and cheeses. Makes about 1½ cups.

Favorite recipe from **Wisconsin Milk Marketing Board**©

Fluffy Fruit Dip

Deviled Egg Pâté

6 hard-cooked eggs
¼ cup mayonnaise
1½ teaspoons prepared mustard
1 teaspoon lemon juice
½ teaspoon Worcestershire sauce
¼ teaspoon salt
⅛ teaspoon pepper
Assorted crackers

Separate egg yolks from whites. Place yolks in medium bowl; mash with fork. Blend mayonnaise and seasonings. Using spoon, press egg whites through sieve and add to yolk mixture. Blend thoroughly. Refrigerate, covered, until ready to serve. Serve with assorted crackers. Makes about 1½ cups.

Favorite recipe from **American Egg Board**

Strawberry Cream Cheese

1 package (8 ounces) cream cheese, softened
¼ cup strawberry jam
2 teaspoons lemon juice
Assorted crackers
Assorted fruit

Place cream cheese, jam and lemon juice in medium bowl. Beat until light and fluffy. Serve with assorted crackers and fruit. Makes about 1½ cups.

Deviled Egg Pâté

Smoked Sausage Roll-Ups

1 sheet frozen puff pastry, thawed
2 packages (5 ounces each) miniature smoked sausage links*

Preheat oven to 450°F. Cut pastry sheet lengthwise into 3 equal strips, then cut each strip crosswise into ten 1-inch wide strips. Roll each strip of pastry around a sausage. Place roll-ups on broiler pan, seam side down, in center of oven. Reduce oven temperature to 400°F. Bake about 15 minutes, until pastry is golden. Makes 30 appetizers.

*1 package (12 ounces) smoked sausage links may be substituted. Cut each link into 4 pieces.

Favorite recipe from **National Live Stock and Meat Board**

Dilly Dip

1 cup dairy sour cream
1 cup mayonnaise
1 to 2 tablespoons milk
1 tablespoon dried parsley
1 tablespoon dried minced onion
1 teaspoon dried dill weed, crushed
Assorted vegetables for dippers

Combine sour cream, mayonnaise, milk, parsley, minced onion and dill weed in small bowl; mix until well blended. Refrigerate, covered, at least 1 hour to blend flavors. Serve with assorted vegetables. Makes about 2 cups.

Favorite recipe from **Wisconsin Milk Marketing Board**©

Cracker Spread

¼ teaspoon unflavored gelatin
1 tablespoon water
½ cup HELLMANN'S® or BEST FOODS® Real Mayonnaise
1 tablespoon chopped parsley (optional)
Assorted crackers
Toppings*

Sprinkle gelatin over water in small saucepan; let stand 1 minute to soften. Stir over medium heat until dissolved. Stir in mayonnaise and parsley. Spread thinly on crackers. Garnish with any of the suggested toppings to make canapés. Refrigerate, covered, up to 3 hours. Makes ½ cup spread.

***Toppings:** Cucumber slices, ripe or green olive slices, tiny shrimp, caviar, pimiento, chopped nuts or parsley or watercress sprigs.

Fancy Franks on Rye

2 packages (5 ounces each) miniature frankfurters
½ cup pimiento cheese spread
16 slices party-size pumpernickel or rye bread, cut crosswise into halves

With sharp knife, cut frankfurters almost through into 16 sections. Spread ½ teaspoon of the cheese spread on each piece of bread. Place 1 frankfurter on each piece of bread, curving slightly. Arrange on broiler pan. Broil, 4 inches from heat, 10 to 12 minutes. Makes 32 appetizers.

Favorite recipe from **National Live Stock and Meat Board**

Turkey Veronica

1 pound unsliced cooked turkey breast, cut into 1-inch cubes
32 seedless green grapes
1 cup Roquefort or creamy Caesar dressing

Place 1 turkey cube and 1 grape on party pick. Repeat with remaining turkey and grapes. Arrange on serving platter around bowl of salad dressing for dipping. Makes 32 appetizers.

Ham and Melon on Party Picks

1 ripe cantaloupe, cut into halves, seeded
½ pound lean ready-to-eat ham steak or unsliced Canadian bacon, cut into 1-inch cubes

Make melon balls using small melon baller or cut melon into quarters and slice into 1-inch cubes. Place 1 melon ball and 1 ham cube on party pick. Repeat with remaining melon and ham. To serve, arrange on platter. Makes 16 servings.

Franks and Apples on Skewers

4 unpared red apples
1 pound turkey or chicken frankfurters, cut into 1-inch pieces

Soak 32 small bamboo skewers in water 10 minutes. Core apples and cut each into 8 wedges. Arrange 1 apple wedge and 1 frankfurter piece on each skewer. Arrange skewers on broiler pan. Broil, 4 inches from heat, just until frankfurters are brown and apples are crisp-tender. Makes 32 appetizers.

Low-Cal Confetti Dip

2 cups low-fat cottage cheese
2 tablespoons lemon juice
Milk
¼ cup finely chopped red bell pepper
2 tablespoons finely chopped green bell pepper
4 green onions with tops, finely chopped
2 tablespoons finely chopped parsley
1 clove garlic, minced (optional)
Salt
Assorted crackers or vegetables for dippers

Place cottage cheese and lemon juice in blender or food processor. Cover and process until smooth and creamy. Pour mixture into medium bowl. Stir in enough milk to make mixture the consistency for dipping. Stir in peppers, onions, parsley and garlic. Season to taste with salt. Serve with assorted crackers or vegetables. Makes 2½ cups.

Top: Turkey Veronica
Left: Franks and Apples on Skewers
Right: Ham and Melon on Party Picks

Creamy Nut Truffles

1 cup semisweet chocolate
    pieces
½ cup whipping cream
¼ cup butter or margarine,
    softened
1 cup RICE CHEX® Brand Cereal,
    crushed to make ⅓ cup
1 egg white
¾ cup hazelnuts, finely chopped
1⅓ cups powdered sugar
1 tablespoon Grand Marnier
    liqueur
3 cups RICE CHEX® Brand
    Cereal, crushed to make
    1½ cups

Butter 8×8-inch baking pan; set
aside. Heat chocolate pieces and
cream in heavy, medium saucepan
over low heat until melted and
smooth, stirring constantly. Remove
from heat; cool slightly. Stir in butter.
Add the ⅓ cup cereal, the egg white
and nuts. Stir in sugar and liqueur;
mix well. Pour into pan. Freeze 3
hours or until firm. Place remaining
1½ cups cereal in shallow dish. Shape
rounded teaspoons of the chocolate
mixture into balls. (Refreeze
chocolate mixture as needed to keep
firm.) Roll balls in cereal to coat.
Refrigerate covered. Let stand at
room temperature 15 minutes before
serving. Makes 48 truffles.

Italian-Flavored Shrimp Dip

1 cup dairy sour cream
**1 package (3 ounces) cream
    cheese, softened**
**½ package Italian salad dressing
    mix (about 1 tablespoon)**
2 teaspoons lemon juice
**1 can (4½ ounces) tiny shrimp,
    rinsed, drained**
**⅓ cup finely chopped green bell
    pepper**
Melba toast rounds
Assorted vegetables for dippers

Combine sour cream and cream
cheese in small bowl; beat until fluffy.
Beat in salad dressing mix and lemon
juice. Stir in shrimp and pepper.

Refrigerate, covered, at least 1 hour.
Serve with Melba toast rounds and
assorted vegetables. Makes about 2½
cups.

Favorite recipe from **Wisconsin Milk
Marketing Board**©

Piña Pepper Spread

**1 can (8 ounces) DOLE® crushed
    pineapple, drained**
½ cup bottled taco sauce
**1 package (8 ounces) cream
    cheese, softened**
Taco chips or crackers

Combine pineapple and taco sauce in
small bowl. Place cream cheese on
serving plate in block or cut into
individual servings. Spoon pineapple
mixture over top. Serve with taco
chips or crackers. Makes 4 servings.

Piña Pepper Spread

Layered Taco Dip

    1 **cup dairy sour cream**
    4 **ounces cream cheese, softened**
  ⅔ **cup bottled taco sauce**
1½ **cups torn lettuce**
  ⅓ **cup chopped green bell pepper**
  ¼ **cup chopped onion**
  ¾ **cup (3 ounces) shredded**
      Wisconsin Cheddar cheese
  ¾ **cup (3 ounces) shredded**
      Wisconsin Monterey Jack
      cheese
    1 **medium tomato, chopped**
      Tortilla chips

Combine sour cream and cream cheese in small bowl; beat until smooth. Spread mixture into 8-inch circle on large platter. Spread taco sauce over cream cheese mixture. Layer with lettuce, pepper, onion, Cheddar cheese and Monterey Jack cheese. Sprinkle tomato over top. Refrigerate, covered, up to 1 hour. Serve with tortilla chips. Makes 8 to 10 servings.

Favorite recipe from **Wisconsin Milk Marketing Board**©

Toasty Onion Sticks

  ⅓ **cup LIPTON® Onion Butter (see**
      following recipe)
  12 **slices white bread**

Prepare LIPTON® Onion Butter. Trim crust from bread. Spread onion butter on bread; cut each slice into 5 strips. Arrange strips on ungreased baking sheet. Bake in preheated 375°F oven 10 minutes or until golden. Makes 5 dozen appetizers.

Onion Party Puffs

  ⅓ **cup LIPTON® Onion Butter**
      (recipe follows)
    1 **package (8 ounces) refrigerator**
      biscuits

Prepare LIPTON® Onion Butter. Cut each biscuit into 4 sections. Arrange on ungreased baking sheet; dot with onion butter. Bake in preheated 400°F oven 8 minutes or until golden. Makes 40 puffs.

Lipton® Onion Butter: Thoroughly blend 1 envelope LIPTON® Onion Soup Mix with ½ pound butter or margarine in medium bowl. Refrigerate, covered, any unused portion. Use on baked potatoes and cooked vegetables. Makes 1¼ cups.

Cottage Guacamole Dip

    1 **avocado, cut into halves**
    1 **cup low-fat cottage cheese**
  ¼ **cup chopped parsley**
    1 **small onion, cut into quarters**
    1 **tablespoon lime juice**
  ½ **teaspoon garlic salt**
      Assorted vegetables for dippers

Place avocado, cheese, parsley, onion, lime juice and garlic salt in blender or food processor. Cover and process until smooth. Transfer to serving bowl. Refrigerate, covered, until serving time. Serve with assorted vegetables. Makes about 2 cups.

Frozen Margaritas (page 78),
Layered Taco Dip

Easy Beef Tortilla Pizzas

- 1 pound ground beef
- 1 medium onion, chopped
- 1 teaspoon dried oregano, crushed
- 1 teaspoon salt
- 4 large flour tortillas (10-inch diameter)
- 4 teaspoons olive oil
- 1 medium tomato, seeded, chopped
  Greek or Mexican Toppings (recipes follow)

Cook and stir ground beef and onion in large skillet over medium-high heat until beef loses pink color. Pour off drippings. Sprinkle oregano and salt over beef, stirring to combine. Place tortillas on 2 large baking sheets. Lightly brush surface of each tortilla with oil. Bake in preheated 400°F oven 3 minutes. Divide beef mixture evenly over tops of tortillas; divide tomato and desired topping over beef mixture. Bake at 400°F 12 to 14 minutes, rearranging baking sheets halfway through cooking time. Makes 4 servings.

Greek Topping: Combine 1 teaspoon dried basil, crushed, ½ teaspoon lemon pepper, 4 ounces crumbled Feta cheese and ¼ cup grated Parmesan cheese in small bowl.

Mexican Topping: Combine 1 teaspoon dried cilantro, crushed, ½ teaspoon crushed dried red chilies, 1 cup (4 ounces) shredded Monterey Jack or Cheddar cheese and ⅓ cup sliced ripe olives in small bowl.

Favorite recipe from **National Live Stock and Meat Board**

Baked Swiss Cheese Fondue

2 cups (8 ounces) shredded aged
　Swiss cheese
½ cup dry white wine
2 tablespoons all-purpose flour
1 teaspoon Dijon-style mustard
　Pinch ground nutmeg
　Assorted vegetables and/or
　French bread chunks for
　dippers

Combine cheese, wine, flour and mustard in 1-quart ovenproof serving dish.* Bake in preheated 425°F oven until cheese bubbles and melts completely, about 20 minutes. Remove from oven and stir. Sprinkle nutmeg over top. Serve hot with assorted vegetables and/or French bread chunks. Makes about 6 servings.

*Fondue may be prepared up to this point and then refrigerated, covered, up to 24 hours.

Vegetable Dip

1 cup low-fat cottage cheese
2 tablespoons finely chopped
　green bell pepper
2 tablespoons finely chopped
　onion
2 tablespoons finely chopped
　radishes
¼ teaspoon celery salt
　Assorted vegetables for dippers

Drain cottage cheese, reserving liquid. Place drained cottage cheese in blender or food processor. (Add 1 to 2 teaspoons of the reserved liquid for easier blending.) Cover and process until smooth. Transfer mixture to small bowl; stir in pepper, onion, radishes and celery salt. Refrigerate, covered, at least 1 hour to allow flavors to blend. Serve with assorted vegetables. Makes 1¼ cups.

Favorite recipe from **Wisconsin Milk Marketing Board©**

Mexi-Beef Bites

1 pound ground beef
1 cup (4 ounces) shredded
　Cheddar cheese
1 cup (4 ounces) shredded
　Monterey Jack cheese
1 can (4 ounces) chopped green
　chilies, drained
½ cup bottled green taco or
　enchilada sauce
2 large eggs, beaten
　Tortilla chips (optional)

Cook and stir beef in large skillet over medium-high heat until beef loses pink color. Pour off drippings. Stir in cheeses, chilies, taco sauce and eggs. Transfer mixture to 8×8-inch baking pan. Bake at 350°F 35 to 40 minutes or until knife inserted in center comes out clean and top is golden brown. Cool in pan 15 minutes. Cut into 36 squares. Serve with tortilla chips. Makes 36 appetizers.

Favorite recipe from **National Live Stock and Meat Board**

PARTY SNACKS

Chili con Queso

- 2 tablespoons CRISCO® Oil
- ¼ cup minced onion
- 1 can (7½ ounces) tomatoes, drained, finely chopped
- 1 can (4 ounces) chopped green chilies, undrained
- ¼ teaspoon salt
- 2 cups (8 ounces) shredded Cheddar or Monterey Jack cheese
- ⅓ cup whipping cream
  Nacho chips

Heat oil in 1-quart saucepan over medium-high heat. Add onion. Cook and stir until onion is tender. Add tomatoes, chilies and salt. Stir to blend and break apart tomatoes. Heat to a boil. Reduce heat to medium-low. Cook 15 minutes; stir occasionally. Remove from heat. Stir in cheese and cream. Cook over low heat until cheese melts, stirring constantly. Transfer to serving bowl. Serve with nacho chips. Makes about 1¾ cups.

Open-Faced Reubens

- **1 box (6 ounces) rye Melba toast rounds**
- **¼ pound thinly sliced cooked corned beef, cut into 1½-inch squares**
- **1 can (8 ounces) sauerkraut, rinsed, drained, chopped**
- **1 cup (4 ounces) shredded Wisconsin Swiss cheese**
- **2 teaspoons prepared mustard Caraway seeds**

Arrange Melba toast rounds on baking sheets. Top each with 1 beef square and 1 teaspoon sauerkraut. Combine cheese and mustard in small bowl; spoon about 1 teaspoon on top of sauerkraut. Sprinkle with caraway seeds. Bake at 350°F 5 minutes or until cheese melts. Makes about 48 appetizers.

Microwave Directions: Arrange 8 Melba toast rounds around edge and 2 rounds in center of microwave-safe plate lined with paper towel. Finish assembling as directed. Microwave, uncovered, at 50% power 1 to 2 minutes or until cheese melts, turning plate once. Repeat with remaining ingredients.

Favorite recipe from **Wisconsin Milk Marketing Board**©

Individual Party Pizzas

8 ounces fresh Italian sausage, casings removed
1 medium onion, chopped
1 clove garlic, minced
1 tablespoon olive oil
1 can (14½ ounces) plum or whole tomatoes, broken up
1 teaspoon dried basil, crushed
1 teaspoon dried oregano, crushed
½ teaspoon dried rosemary, crushed
½ teaspoon salt
2 cans (10 ounces each) refrigerated pizza dough
4 ounces pepperoni, thinly sliced
1 small red or green bell pepper, cut into ½-inch pieces
1 small onion, coarsely chopped
¼ pound mushrooms, sliced
1 can (2¼ ounces) sliced ripe olives, drained
1 jar (6 ounces) marinated, quartered artichokes, drained, cut into halves
Crushed dried red chilies
3 cups (12 ounces) shredded mozzarella cheese
¼ cup grated Parmesan cheese

Place sausage in small skillet; break up. Cook over medium heat until meat loses pink color, stirring constantly. Pour off drippings; set aside.

Cook medium onion and garlic in oil in medium skillet over medium-high heat until onion is tender. Add tomatoes, basil, oregano, rosemary and salt. Reduce heat to low; simmer, uncovered, 30 minutes, stirring occasionally. Cool.

Meanwhile, prepare crusts. Divide dough from each can into 3 pieces (do not unroll). Roll each piece on lightly floured surface into 7-inch circle; prick several times with fork. Arrange on greased baking sheets. Cover; let rest 10 minutes. Again press each piece into 7-inch circle; prick several times with fork. Bake in preheated 425°F oven 12 to 15 minutes.

Spread sauce over each prebaked crust. Divide sausage and ½ of the pepperoni over crusts. Place red pepper, small onion, mushrooms, olives, artichokes and dried red chilies on crusts. Top each with remaining pepperoni and cheeses. Bake in preheated 425°F oven 12 to 14 minutes. Makes 6 servings.

Favorite recipe from **National Live Stock and Meat Board**

Festive Kabob Hors d'Oeuvre

1 package (8 ounces) mozzarella cheese, cut into 1 × ½-inch pieces
¼ pound sliced salami
2 cups cherry tomatoes
2 cups small mushrooms
1 package (9 ounces) frozen artichoke hearts, thawed
1 can (6 ounces) pitted ripe olives
½ cup WISH-BONE® Herbal Italian Dressing
¼ cup dry white wine

Wrap cheese inside salami. On 12 skewers, alternately thread salami rolls, tomatoes, mushrooms, artichokes and olives; place in shallow baking dish. Blend dressing with wine in small bowl. Pour over kabobs. Marinate in refrigerator, covered, at least 4 hours, turning occasionally. Drain marinade before serving. Makes 12 appetizers.

Individual Party Pizzas

Sausage Pineapple Pizza

- 2 cloves garlic, pressed or minced
- 1 cup pizza sauce
- 2 teaspoons dried oregano, crushed
- 1 loaf packaged frozen bread dough, thawed
- 1 cup chopped green bell pepper
- ½ cup chopped green onion
- 1 pound Italian sausage, cooked, crumbled
- 4 cups (16 ounces) shredded mozzarella or Cheddar cheese
- ¼ cup grated Parmesan cheese
- 4 cans (8 ounces each) DOLE® Pineapple Tidbits in Juice, drained

Combine garlic, pizza sauce and oregano in medium bowl; set aside. Roll out ½ the dough on lightly floured surface to fit 12-inch pizza pan or 13×9×2-inch baking pan. Fit dough in greased pan. If using 13×9×2-inch baking pan, press dough 1 inch up sides of pan to resemble deep-dish pizza. Repeat with remaining dough.

Spread both doughs with pizza sauce mixture. Top with pepper, onion, sausage, cheeses and pineapple. Bake in preheated 500°F oven 12 to 15 minutes or until bubbly and crust is browned. Makes 12 servings.

Peanut Butter Rice Snacks

1 cup light corn syrup
½ cup granulated sugar
½ cup packed brown sugar
1 cup crunchy peanut butter
6 cups RICE CHEX® Brand Cereal

Line 9×9-inch pan with waxed paper. Combine corn syrup and sugars in large saucepan. Cook over medium heat just until mixture comes to a boil, stirring frequently. Remove from heat. Stir in peanut butter until well combined. Gradually add cereal, stirring until all pieces are evenly coated. Turn into prepared pan. Refrigerate 15 minutes or until firm. Cut into squares. Store covered. Makes about 16 squares.

Herbed Salmon Ball

1 can (15½ ounces) red salmon
1 package (8 ounces) cream cheese, softened
1 clove garlic, minced
½ cup small-curd cottage cheese
¼ cup minced onion
1 teaspoon dried fines herbes, crushed
½ teaspoon dried thyme, crushed
1 cup chopped parsley
½ cup chopped walnuts
Assorted crackers

Drain salmon; remove skin. Place salmon in small bowl; mash bones with fork. Combine cream cheese, garlic, cottage cheese, onion, fines herbes and thyme in medium bowl until well blended. Stir in salmon. Form mixture into a ball. Refrigerate, covered, 3 hours. Mixture will be soft. Roll in parsley and walnuts. Serve with assorted crackers. Makes 4 servings.

Peanut Butter Rice Snacks

Kamaaina Sparerib-lettes

2 pounds lean pork spareribs, cracked
1 can (8 ounces) DOLE® Crushed Pineapple in Syrup
½ cup catsup
¼ cup wine vinegar
3 tablespoons packed brown sugar
3 tablespoons soy sauce
1 teaspoon ground ginger
½ teaspoon dry mustard
¼ teaspoon garlic powder

Have your butcher cut the spareribs across the bones to make short lengths. Cut apart into single ribs. Arrange close together in single layer in baking pan. Cover tightly with aluminum foil. Bake at 350°F 1 hour. Uncover and pour off drippings. Drain 1 tablespoon of the syrup from pineapple; combine the 1 tablespoon syrup with the catsup, vinegar, sugar, soy sauce, ginger, mustard and garlic powder in small bowl. Spoon sauce over ribs. Bake 30 minutes more. Spoon remaining undrained pineapple over ribs; continue baking 15 minutes more or until ribs are tender and glazed. Makes about 2 dozen appetizers.

Kahlúa Picadillo Filling

¼ cup raisins, finely chopped
4 tablespoons KAHLÚA®, divided
⅓ cup finely chopped onion
1 tablespoon vegetable oil
½ cup canned green chilies, finely
    chopped
2 tablespoons vinegar, divided
1 teaspoon salt
⅛ teaspoon pepper
1 pound ground chuck beef
1 can (14½ ounces) tomatoes,
    chopped
⅓ cup pine nuts or slivered
    almonds (optional)
    Taco chips

Combine raisins and 3 tablespoons of the KAHLÚA® in small bowl; set aside. Cook and stir onion in oil in large skillet over medium-high heat until onion is transparent. Add chilies, 1 tablespoon of the vinegar, the salt and pepper. Add beef and raisin mixture; mix thoroughly. Lightly brown meat over medium heat, breaking up meat as it cooks. Add tomatoes and remaining 1 tablespoon each KAHLÚA® and vinegar. Bring to a boil over high heat. Reduce heat to low; simmer, uncovered, until thickened, about 15 minutes. Stir in nuts. Serve with taco chips. Makes 3¼ cups.

Mexican Egg Pockets

4 eggs
¼ cup milk
2 teaspoons chopped chives
¼ teaspoon salt
1 tablespoon butter
2 pita breads, cut into halves
1 cup chopped tomatoes
¼ cup chopped green bell pepper
¼ cup chopped green onions with
    tops
½ cup (2 ounces) shredded
    Cheddar cheese
¼ cup bottled taco sauce

Beat eggs, milk, chives and salt in small bowl with fork. Heat butter in 8-inch skillet over medium heat until just hot enough to sizzle a drop of water. Pour in egg mixture. As mixture begins to set, gently draw inverted pancake turner completely across bottom and sides of pan, forming large soft curds. Continue until eggs are thickened, but still moist.* Do not stir constantly.

Place pita halves upright in loaf pan. Fill each half with ¼ of the cooked eggs, the tomatoes, pepper and onions. Sprinkle with cheese. Bake in preheated 350°F oven just until cheese melts, about 5 minutes. Top each pita half with 1 tablespoon of the taco sauce. Serve immediately. Makes 4 servings.

*It is better to remove scrambled eggs from pan when they are slightly underdone. Heat retained in egg completes the cooking.

Favorite recipe from **American Egg Board**

Mexican Hero

⅓ cup bottled taco sauce
1 egg, beaten
1 teaspoon seasoned salt
1 pound lean ground beef
1½ cups CORN CHEX® Brand
    Cereal, crushed to make
    ½ cup
1 loaf (16 to 18 inches) French
    bread, split
1 medium tomato, chopped
½ cup shredded lettuce
½ cup (2 ounces) shredded
    Cheddar cheese

Combine taco sauce, egg and salt in
medium bowl. Stir in beef and cereal;
mix well. Shape into 4 oval patties.
Arrange on broiler pan. Broil, 4
inches from heat, 10 to 12 minutes or
until desired doneness, turning over
once. Arrange on split loaf. Top with
tomato, lettuce and cheese. To serve,
place top on loaf; slice crosswise into
4 sandwiches. Serve with additional
taco sauce if desired. Makes 4
servings.

Layered Nacho Dip

1 medium avocado, mashed
    (about 1 cup)
2 teaspoons lemon juice
¼ teaspoon hot pepper sauce
2 cups dairy sour cream, divided
1 package (8 ounces) cream
    cheese, softened
1 envelope LIPTON® Nacho
    Cheese Recipe Soup Mix
Assorted vegetables for dippers

Combine avocado, lemon juice and
hot pepper sauce in small bowl.
Combine 1 cup of the sour cream, the
cream cheese and nacho cheese soup
mix in blender or food processor.
Cover and process until blended.
Layer ½ of the nacho mixture, then
the avocado mixture, remaining 1 cup
sour cream and the remaining nacho
mixture in 5-cup bowl. Refrigerate,
covered, until chilled. Garnish as
desired. Serve with assorted
vegetables. Makes about 4 cups.

Mexican Hero

Sausage Strudel Hors d'Oeuvre

½ pound sweet Italian sausage
    links, casings removed
½ cup chopped green bell pepper
½ cup thinly sliced mushrooms
¼ cup chopped onion
2 cloves garlic, finely chopped
1 egg, slightly beaten
3 tablespoons tomato paste
3 tablespoons grated Parmesan
    cheese
½ teaspoon dried oregano,
    crushed
1½ cups (6 ounces) shredded
    mozzarella cheese
12 sheets phyllo
    Butter or margarine, melted
½ cup dry bread crumbs

Cook sausage, pepper, mushrooms, onion and garlic in medium skillet over medium-high heat 8 minutes or until sausage is done; set aside. Blend egg, tomato paste, Parmesan cheese and oregano in medium bowl. Stir in sausage mixture and mozzarella cheese. Unfold phyllo sheets; cover with plastic wrap, then damp cloth. Remove 4 sheets at a time and place on second damp cloth covered with plastic wrap. Brush 1 sheet with butter, then sprinkle with 2 teaspoons of the bread crumbs. Repeat to make 4 layers. On top sheet, spoon ⅓ of the sausage mixture along narrow side, ¼ inch from edge. Fold in long sides about ½ inch. Roll up, jelly-roll style, starting at narrow end. Place on greased baking sheet, seam side down; brush with butter. Repeat with remaining ingredients. Bake in preheated 350°F oven 20 minutes or until golden. To serve, cut with serrated knife into 1½-inch slices. Makes about 30 appetizers.

Top: Layered Nacho Dip
Bottom: Sausage Strudel
Hors d'Oeuvre

Sausage Antipasto Platter

    Pesto Spread (recipe follows)
1 large tomato
6 ounces thinly sliced Genoa
    salami
6 ounces thinly sliced ham
    cappicola
6 ounces thinly sliced pepperoni
1 loaf (8 ounces) French bread,
    cut into ¼-inch slices
1 pound unpared cooked new
    potatoes, cut into ¼-inch
    slices
4 ounces pea pods, trimmed,
    strings removed
1 red bell pepper, cut into strips
1 small zucchini, cut diagonally
    into ¼-inch slices
4 ounces mushrooms, sliced
½ cup dry cured olives (optional)

Prepare Pesto Spread. Cut ½-inch slice from top of tomato; zigzag edge. Scoop out pulp. Fill tomato with Pesto Spread; place in center of large serving platter. Arrange remaining ingredients around tomato. To serve, spread slices of bread or potatoes with Pesto Spread and top with sliced meat and vegetables. Makes 8 servings.

Pesto Spread: Combine ¾ cup tightly packed fresh basil leaves, 2 teaspoons crushed fresh rosemary or ¾ teaspoon dried rosemary, crushed, ¼ cup tightly packed Italian parsley and 2 quartered garlic cloves in food processor. Cover and process until blended. Add ⅓ cup French bread crumbs, ¼ cup grated Parmesan cheese, 1 teaspoon lemon juice, ½ teaspoon salt and dash pepper. With motor running, slowly pour in ⅓ cup light cream and ¼ cup olive oil through feed tube. Process until blended. Pour into small bowl. Refrigerate, covered, 1½ to 2 hours to blend flavors. Makes about 1 cup.

Favorite recipe from **National Live Stock and Meat Board**

Colorful Beef Spread

6 ounces lean cooked beef, cut
    into 1-inch pieces
½ teaspoon salt
⅛ teaspoon pepper
1 small zucchini, cut into 8 pieces
1 small onion, cut into quarters
¼ red bell pepper, cut into
    4 pieces
¼ cup low-calorie creamy
    cucumber dressing
1 medium cucumber, sliced
¾ cup red bell pepper squares
4 ounces pea pods, trimmed,
    strings removed

Place beef, salt and pepper in food processor. Cover and process until coarsely chopped, about 5 seconds. Add zucchini, onion and the 4 red pepper pieces; process 15 to 20 seconds, using pulse or on and off motion. Add dressing and process 5 seconds or until mixture is blended. Transfer to serving bowl. Refrigerate, covered, at least 1 hour. Spread on cucumber slices, red pepper squares and pea pods. Makes 1¼ cups.

Favorite recipe from **National Live Stock and Meat Board**

Sausage Antipasto Platter

OPEN HOUSE

Stuffed Cucumber Slices

- 1 large cucumber
- 1 package (3 ounces) cream cheese, softened
- 1 tablespoon blue cheese, crumbled
- 1 teaspoon grated onion
- 2 teaspoons minced parsley
- ½ teaspoon dried dill weed
- 20 to 25 pimiento strips

Score cucumber with tines of fork. Cut 1-inch slice from 1 end of cucumber. Using an iced tea spoon, scoop seeds from inside of cucumber.

Stand cucumber on cut end on paper towel to drain, about 10 minutes.

Combine cream cheese, blue cheese, onion, parsley and dill weed in small bowl. Spoon mixture into hollowed-out center of cucumber. Wrap in plastic wrap. Refrigerate 3 to 4 hours. Slice crosswise into ¼-inch slices. Garnish slices with pimiento strips. Makes 20 to 25 appetizers.

Crispy Crab Wontons

- 1 package (8 ounces) cream cheese, softened
- 1 teaspoon Worcestershire sauce

1 teaspoon dried parsley flakes
½ teaspoon dry mustard
¼ teaspoon seasoned salt
1 can (6½ ounces) crabmeat,
   drained, picked over
1 package (16 ounces) wonton
   wrappers
½ cup milk
5 cups RICE CHEX® Brand
   Cereal, crushed to make
   1⅔ cups
Vegetable oil for frying

Beat cream cheese in large bowl until fluffy. Add Worcestershire sauce, parsley, mustard and seasoned salt; mix well. Fold in crabmeat. Place 1 teaspoon of the crab filling in center of each wonton wrapper. Moisten edges with milk; fold in half to form triangle. Bring opposite points

together, pinching edges to seal. Dip wontons in milk. Place cereal in shallow dish; roll wontons in cereal to coat.*

Meanwhile, heat 2 inches oil in heavy, large saucepan over medium-high heat until oil is 375°F; adjust heat to maintain temperature. Fry wontons, a few at a time, 2 to 3 minutes or until golden brown. Drain on paper towels. Serve immediately. Makes 50 appetizers.

*Wontons may be refrigerated overnight before frying or frozen, thawed and fried just before serving.

Left to right: Stuffed Cucumber Slices, Crispy Crab Wontons, Port Cheddar Cheese Spread (page 60)

Easy Vegetable Squares

2 packages (8 ounces each)
    refrigerated crescent rolls
1 package (8 ounces) cream
    cheese, softened
1 package (3 ounces) cream
    cheese, softened
⅓ cup mayonnaise
1 teaspoon dried dill weed,
    crushed
1 teaspoon buttermilk salad
    dressing mix
3 cups toppings*
1 cup (4 ounces) shredded
    Wisconsin Cheddar,
    mozzarella or Monterey Jack
    cheese

Unroll crescent rolls and pat into
15½×10½×2-inch baking pan. Bake
according to package directions. Cool
on wire rack.

Meanwhile, blend cream cheese,
mayonnaise, dill weed and salad
dressing mix in small bowl. Spread
evenly over crust. Sprinkle with
desired toppings, then shredded
cheese. To serve, cut into squares.
Makes 32 appetizers.

*Toppings: Finely chopped broccoli,
cauliflower or green pepper; seeded
and chopped tomato; thinly sliced
green onion, ripe olives or celery; or
shredded carrot.

Favorite recipe from **Wisconsin Milk
Marketing Board**©

Port Cheddar Cheese Spread

4 cups (1 pound) shredded sharp
    Cheddar cheese
¼ cup butter or margarine,
    softened
¼ cup dairy sour cream
2 tablespoons port wine
¼ teaspoon ground mace
⅛ teaspoon ground red pepper
1 cup chopped toasted walnuts
    Assorted vegetables for dippers
    Assorted crackers

Combine cheese, butter, sour cream,
wine, mace and ground red pepper in
food processor. Cover and process
until smooth. Mix in walnuts.
Refrigerate, covered, several days to
allow flavors to mellow. Soften
slightly at room temperature before
serving. Serve with assorted
vegetables and crackers. Makes about
3 cups.

Favorite recipe from **Walnut Marketing
Board**

Mini Ham Sandwiches

1 jar (7 ounces) Italian-style
    roasted peppers, drained
2 jars (6 ounces each) marinated
    artichoke hearts, drained
8 tablespoons butter or
    margarine, softened
2 tablespoons Dijon-style
    mustard
1 loaf (1 pound) party-size rye
    bread
1¼ pounds thinly sliced cooked
    ham

Cut roasted peppers lengthwise into
2×¼-inch strips. Cut each artichoke
heart in half. Beat butter and
mustard in small bowl until blended.
Spread butter mixture on 1 side of
each bread slice. Divide ham on
buttered sides of bread. Place 1
artichoke piece on each sandwich,
then crisscross 2 roasted pepper
strips on top. Makes about 40
sandwiches.

Appeteaser Cheese Pie

1½ cups Cheddar cheese cracker crumbs
⅓ cup butter or margarine, melted
¾ cup LIPTON® California Dip (recipe follows)
¼ cup cold milk
1 envelope KNOX® Unflavored Gelatine
¾ cup milk, heated to boiling
1 package (3 ounces) cream cheese, softened
1 teaspoon Worcestershire sauce
¾ cup chopped vegetables*
Olive slices for garnish
Pimiento strips for garnish

Combine cracker crumbs with butter in medium bowl. Press ½ of the mixture onto bottom of 8- or 9-inch pie pan; refrigerate. Reserve remaining crumb mixture. Prepare LIPTON® California Dip. Place cold milk in 5-cup blender. Sprinkle gelatine over milk; let stand 3 to 4 minutes. Add hot milk. Cover and process at low speed until gelatine is completely dissolved, about 2 minutes. Add cream cheese, California Dip and Worcestershire sauce; process at high speed until blended. Stir in chopped vegetables. Turn into prepared crust; top with reserved crumb mixture. Refrigerate until firm. Garnish with olive slices and pimiento strips. Makes about 10 servings.

*Suggested Vegetables: Use any combination of the following: carrot, celery, cucumber, green bell pepper or tomato.

Lipton® California Dip: Blend 1 envelope LIPTON® Onion Soup Mix with 2 cups dairy sour cream in medium bowl. Refrigerate covered. Makes about 2 cups.

Sauerkraut Balls

Mustard Sauce (see page 18)
1 tablespoon CRISCO® Oil
⅓ cup finely chopped onion
2 tablespoons all-purpose flour
1 can (27 ounces) sauerkraut,
   rinsed, squeezed dry
6 ounces bulk pork sausage
1 egg, slightly beaten
1 egg
1 tablespoon milk
½ cup seasoned fine dry bread
   crumbs
CRISCO® Oil for frying

Prepare Mustard Sauce. Heat 1 tablespoon oil in small skillet over medium heat. Cook and stir onion in hot oil until tender. Remove from heat; stir in flour. Transfer mixture to medium bowl. Add sauerkraut, sausage and the slightly beaten egg; mix well. Refrigerate, covered, at least 1 hour.

Mix remaining egg and milk in small bowl. Place bread crumbs in shallow dish. Shape sauerkraut mixture into 1-inch balls. Dip balls in egg mixture, then roll in crumbs.

Heat 2 to 3 inches oil in heavy, large saucepan over medium high heat until oil is 350°F; adjust heat to maintain temperature. Fry, a few balls at a time, 3 to 4 minutes or until deep golden brown, turning over halfway through frying. Drain on paper towels.* Serve hot with Mustard Sauce. Makes 3 dozen appetizers.

*To make 1 day ahead, prepare and fry as directed. Cool. Refrigerate covered. Reheat in single layer on baking sheet in preheated 400°F oven 8 to 10 minutes or until hot.

Simply Smashing Ham Ribbons

¼ cup WISH-BONE® Deluxe
  French Dressing
¼ cup apricot preserves
⅛ teaspoon dry mustard
1 loaf thinly sliced white bread
  (about 24 slices)
1 loaf thinly sliced whole wheat
  bread (about 24 slices)
  Butter or margarine, softened
12 thin slices cooked ham

Blend dressing, preserves and mustard in small bowl. Trim crust from breads. Butter 12 slices of the white bread and 12 slices of the whole wheat bread. Spread each of the remaining 12 slices whole wheat bread with 2 teaspoons of the dressing mixture. (The remaining 12 slices white bread stay plain.)

To assemble the 12 sandwich stacks, layer as follows: Place buttered white bread, buttered side up; whole wheat bread, dressing side up; unbuttered white bread; ham slice; buttered whole wheat bread, buttered side down. Wrap in waxed paper or plastic wrap and chill. To serve, cut each stack lengthwise into thirds, then in half crosswise. Makes 72 appetizers.

Nutty Cream Cheese Spirals

⅔ cup WISH-BONE® Russian
  Dressing
1 package (8 ounces) cream
  cheese, softened
1 cup finely chopped walnuts
1 loaf (16 ounces) unsliced white
  bread, cut lengthwise into
  8 slices

Combine dressing, cream cheese and walnuts in medium bowl until well blended. Trim crust from bread; flatten slightly with rolling pin. Spread 3 tablespoons of the dressing mixture on each slice of bread; roll up jelly-roll style. Wrap in waxed paper or plastic wrap and chill. To serve, cut into ½-inch slices. Makes about 60 appetizers.

Stuffed Mushrooms Italiano

1 pound large mushrooms
¼ cup WISH-BONE® Italian or
    Caesar Dressing·
1 cup fresh bread crumbs
¼ cup grated Parmesan cheese
1 tablespoon finely chopped
    parsley

Remove and finely chop mushroom stems. Combine dressing, bread crumbs, cheese, parsley and chopped mushroom stems in medium bowl. Fill each mushroom cap with bread crumb mixture; arrange in shallow baking dish. Add water to barely cover bottom of dish. Bake in preheated 350°F oven 20 minutes. Makes about 24 appetizers.

Londonderry Watercress Rounds

2 ounces cream cheese, softened
¼ cup WISH-BONE® Ranch·
    Dressing
½ cup chopped watercress
30 slices thinly sliced white bread
    Watercress sprigs (optional)

Blend cream cheese and dressing in small bowl. Stir in watercress. Using 1½-inch biscuit cutter, cut 120 rounds from bread. Cut ½-inch circle from center of ½ of the rounds to form "doughnut" shape. Spread remaining rounds with dressing mixture, then top with "doughnut" rounds. Wrap in plastic wrap; refrigerate until chilled. Garnish with watercress sprigs. Makes 60 appetizers.

Southwestern Salsa

1 pound tomatoes, chopped, or
    1 can (14½ ounces) tomatoes,
    drained, chopped
1 large green chili, finely
    chopped, or 1 can (4 ounces)
    diced green chilies, drained
4 green onions with tops, finely
    chopped
2 tablespoons lemon juice
2 to 4 tablespoons finely chopped
    cilantro
    Hot pepper sauce
    Salt
    Corn chips

Combine tomatoes, chili, onions and lemon juice in medium bowl. Add cilantro. Stir in hot pepper sauce and salt, to taste. Refrigerate, covered, about 1 hour to blend flavors. Serve with corn chips. Makes 4 cups.

Tuna-Egg Dip Appetizer

1 can (6½ ounces) solid white
    tuna, drained
3 hard-cooked eggs, chopped
¾ cup mayonnaise
¾ cup dairy sour cream
1 tablespoon minced green onion
1 small clove garlic, minced
1 teaspoon paprika
½ teaspoon dried dill weed,
    crushed
    Assorted vegetables for dippers

With fork, flake tuna in medium bowl. Add eggs, mayonnaise, sour cream, onion, garlic, paprika and dill weed. Mix well. Transfer to serving bowl. Serve with assorted vegetables. Makes 2½ cups.

Top to bottom: Simply Smashing Ham Ribbons, Londonderry Watercress Rounds, Stuffed Mushrooms Italiano, Nutty Cream Cheese Spirals

Garden Vegetable Dip

Garden Vegetable Dip

- 1 cup chopped cauliflower
- 1 cup chopped broccoli
- 1 cup chopped carrots
- ½ cup chopped onion
- 2 packages (8 ounces each) cream cheese, softened, cut into cubes
- 1 teaspoon dried dill weed, crushed
- ½ teaspoon ground cumin
- ¼ teaspoon chili powder
- ⅛ teaspoon salt
- 5 to 10 drops hot pepper sauce
  Assorted vegetables for dippers

Combine cauliflower, broccoli, carrots and onion in food processor. Cover and process until finely minced. Add cream cheese, dill weed, cumin, chili powder, salt and hot pepper sauce. Process until well blended. Transfer to serving bowl. Refrigerate, covered, at least 3 hours. Serve with assorted vegetables. Makes about 3½ cups.

Bean Dip

- 2 tablespoons vegetable oil
- 1 small onion, finely chopped
- 1 clove garlic, crushed
- 1 can (15 ounces) refried beans
- 1 can (4 ounces) diced green chilies
- 1 teaspoon chili powder
  Dash hot pepper sauce
- 1 cup (4 ounces) shredded Monterey Jack cheese
  Tortilla chips for dippers

Heat oil in medium saucepan over medium heat. Add onion and garlic. Cook and stir until tender. Stir in refried beans, chilies, chili powder and hot pepper sauce. Heat until bubbly, stirring occasionally. Stir in cheese; heat until melted. Serve hot with tortilla chips. Makes about 2 cups.

Shrimp and Cream Cheese Spread

- 1 package (8 ounces) cream cheese, softened
- 1 tablespoon chili sauce
- 1 tablespoon prepared horseradish
- 2 teaspoons lemon juice
- ⅛ teaspoon white pepper
- ¼ pound peeled, cooked small shrimp, finely chopped
  Assorted crackers

Combine cream cheese, chili sauce, horseradish and lemon juice in medium bowl. Stir in pepper and shrimp. Serve with assorted crackers. Makes about 1½ cups.

Pork Apple Kabobs

- 2 pork blade steaks, cut ¾ inch thick
- ¾ cup apple juice
- ⅓ cup plus 2 tablespoons catsup, divided
- 2 tablespoons soy sauce
- 1 clove garlic, minced
- 1 small green bell pepper, cut into 24 pieces
- 1 large Red Delicious apple
  Lemon juice

Partially freeze steaks; remove bones. Slice into ⅛- to ¼-inch thick strips. Combine apple juice, ⅓ cup of the catsup, the soy sauce and garlic in medium bowl. Place meat in plastic bag; add marinade, turning to coat. Tie bag. Marinate in refrigerator at least 4 hours.

Soak 24 (8-inch) bamboo skewers in water 10 minutes. Remove meat from marinade; reserve marinade. Thread pork strips on skewers by weaving strips back and forth. Place 1 pepper piece on each skewer. Combine the remaining 2 tablespoons catsup with 3 tablespoons of the reserved marinade. Arrange skewers on broiler pan. Broil, 4 inches from heat, 15 to 16 minutes, turning and basting with marinade occasionally. Cut apple into 24 pieces; dip in lemon juice. Place 1 apple piece on each kabob before serving. Makes 24 appetizers.

Favorite recipe from **National Live Stock and Meat Board**

Pork Apple Kabobs

Crunchy Oriental Meatballs

1 can (8 ounces) sliced water chestnuts, drained, finely chopped
1 pound lean ground beef
1 egg, slightly beaten
1 tablespoon cornstarch
½ teaspoon salt
¼ teaspoon black pepper
½ teaspoon Chinese five spice powder
1½ tablespoons cornstarch
1 tablespoon sugar
1½ cups apricot nectar
3 tablespoons white vinegar
1 teaspoon grated fresh ginger
Dash soy sauce
Dash hot pepper sauce
¼ cup finely chopped red bell pepper
3 green onions with tops, chopped

Combine water chestnuts, beef, egg, cornstarch, salt, black pepper and five spice powder in medium bowl. Make meatballs using 1 tablespoonful of the meat mixture for each meatball. Arrange in jelly-roll pan. Bake in preheated 475°F oven 10 to 15 minutes or until brown.

Meanwhile, prepare sauce. Combine cornstarch and sugar in medium saucepan. Gradually stir in apricot nectar. Stir in vinegar, ginger, soy sauce and hot pepper sauce. Cook over medium heat until thickened, stirring constantly. Stir in red pepper and onions; cook 2 minutes more, stirring occasionally. Add browned meatballs. Reduce heat to low; cook 5 minutes more. Spoon into chafing dish. Makes about 35 meatballs.

Hawaiian Chicken Strips

½ cup mayonnaise
1 tablespoon Dijon-style mustard
1 tablespoon honey
4 cups RICE CHEX® Brand Cereal, crushed to make 1⅔ cups
½ cup flaked coconut
1 pound skinless, boneless chicken breasts, cut into ½-inch wide strips
Cherry tomatoes
Pineapple chunks
Green bell pepper chunks

Combine mayonnaise, mustard and honey in shallow dish. Combine cereal and coconut in another shallow dish or large plastic bag. Coat chicken strips, a few at a time, in mayonnaise mixture, then in cereal mixture.* Thread chicken strips on skewers; place cherry tomato, pineapple chunk or pepper chunk on end of each skewer. Arrange on rack in shallow baking pan. Bake in preheated 400°F oven 15 to 20 minutes or until chicken strips are no longer pink in center. Makes 25 to 30 appetizers.

*Chicken strips can be coated a day before serving. Refrigerate covered. Cooking time may need to be increased.

Hawaiian Chicken Strips

Holiday Ham Spread

1 can (20 ounces) DOLE®
    Crushed Pineapple
2 cups diced cooked ham
⅓ cup mayonnaise
¼ cup minced green onions
3 tablespoons Dijon-style
    mustard
2 teaspoons caraway seeds
    Party-size rye or pumpernickel
    bread

Drain pineapple well, pressing out
juice with back of spoon. Process ham
in covered blender or food processor,
a few pieces at a time, until minced.
Combine pineapple, ham,
mayonnaise, onions, mustard and
caraway seeds in medium bowl.
Spread on bread. Garnish as desired.
Makes 8 to 10 servings.

Blue Cheese Pecan Ball

1 package (8 ounces) cream
    cheese, softened
¾ cup (3 ounces) crumbled
    Wisconsin blue cheese
3 tablespoons milk
1 cup chopped pecans
    Snipped parsley
    Pecan halves
    Assorted crackers

Blend cheeses and milk in large bowl
until well blended. Stir in chopped
pecans. Shape into ball. Refrigerate,
covered, until firm. Roll in parsley;
garnish with pecan halves. Serve with
assorted crackers. Makes 1 ball.

Favorite recipe from **Wisconsin Milk
Marketing Board**©

Scandinavian Meatballs with Sour Cream Sauce

1 small (4 ounces) unpared potato
1 medium onion, cut into quarters
¼ cup dry bread crumbs
1 tablespoon milk
1 egg, slightly beaten
1⅛ teaspoon salt, divided
¼ teaspoon plus ⅛ teaspoon
    black pepper, divided
1 pound ground pork
1½ teaspoons butter or margarine
1½ teaspoons all-purpose flour
½ teaspoon dried dill weed
    Dash ground red pepper
¼ cup water
¼ cup white wine
½ cup dairy sour cream
    Fresh dill for garnish

Microwave Directions: Prick potato
with fork several times. Place on
paper towel in microwave oven.
Microwave at High 3 minutes. Wrap
in aluminum foil; let stand 1 minute.
Cut potato into quarters. Place
potato, onion, bread crumbs, milk,
egg, 1 teaspoon of the salt and ¼
teaspoon of the black pepper in food
processor. Cover and process until
smooth. Combine ground pork and
potato mixture in large bowl until
thoroughly mixed. Refrigerate,
covered, 30 minutes. Shape mixture
into 16 meatballs. (Mixture will be
very light and sticky.) Arrange
meatballs in 12×8-inch microwave-
safe baking dish. Cover with plastic
wrap (do not vent). Microwave at
High 4 minutes. Rearrange and turn
meatballs over. Microwave at High 3
minutes. Remove meatballs to
platter; set aside.

Melt butter in 2-cup glass measure at High 15 to 30 seconds. Stir in flour, dill weed, ground red pepper, remaining ⅛ teaspoon salt and remaining ⅛ teaspoon black pepper. Whisk in water and wine. Microwave, uncovered, at High 3 minutes. Place sour cream in microwave-safe bowl. Gradually add hot sauce, stirring constantly to prevent curdling. Microwave at 50% power 1 minute. Pour over meatballs. Garnish with fresh dill. Makes 8 servings.

Favorite recipe from **National Live Stock and Meat Board**

Festive Cheese Ball with Grapes

1 package (8 ounces) cream cheese, softened
1 cup (4 ounces) shredded Cheddar cheese
⅛ teaspoon hot pepper sauce
2 tablespoons chopped walnuts
2 pounds blue, green and red grapes, cut into small clusters

Beat cheeses and hot pepper sauce in small bowl until well blended. Place cheese mixture into 1-quart round bowl lined with plastic wrap. Refrigerate, covered, until firm. Unmold and place in center of serving platter. Remove plastic wrap. Smooth cheese with spatula. Sprinkle with walnuts. Surround with grape clusters. Makes 1½ cups.

Favorite recipe from **National Live Stock and Meat Board**

Souper Quiche Squares

Pastry for single-crust 9-inch pie
2 cans (4 ounces each) sliced mushrooms, drained
1 cup (4 ounces) shredded Swiss or Cheddar cheese
6 eggs, beaten
1 can (10¾ ounces) condensed cream of celery soup
½ cup milk
1 tablespoon instant minced onion
¼ teaspoon dried basil, crushed
⅛ teaspoon pepper

Roll out dough on lightly floured waxed paper to 13×9-inch rectangle. Place dough, paper side up, over 11×7×2-inch baking pan. Remove and discard paper. Fit pastry into pan, gently pressing dough to completely cover bottom and sides of pan. Trim excess pastry.

Sprinkle mushrooms and cheese over pastry. Beat remaining ingredients in medium bowl until blended. Pour into pastry. Bake in preheated 375°F oven 25 to 30 minutes or until knife inserted halfway between center and outside edge comes out clean. Let stand at least 5 minutes before serving. Cut into squares. Serve hot or cold. Makes 24 appetizers.

Favorite recipe from **American Egg Board**

Mushroom Demi-Tarts

- **3 cups RICE CHEX® Brand Cereal, crushed to make ¾ cup**
- **⅔ cup plus 2 tablespoons all-purpose flour, divided**
- **½ teaspoon salt, divided**
- **⅓ cup plus 2 tablespoons butter or margarine, softened, divided**
- **1 package (3 ounces) cream cheese, softened**
- **½ pound mushrooms, coarsely chopped**
- **2 tablespoons minced green onions**
- **½ cup whipping cream**

Combine cereal, ⅔ cup of the flour and ¼ teaspoon of the salt in medium bowl. Combine ⅓ cup of the butter and the cream cheese in small bowl until well blended. Add to cereal mixture, stirring until mixture holds together. Make 22 balls using scant 1 tablespoon of the mixture for each. Place in ungreased 1¾-inch muffin cups. Press against bottoms and sides of cups. Bake in preheated 400°F oven 10 to 12 minutes or until golden brown. Cool in pan on wire rack 10 minutes. Remove tarts from cups. Cool completely on wire rack.

Melt remaining 2 tablespoons butter in medium skillet over medium heat. Stir in mushrooms and onions; cook 5 minutes or until tender, stirring occasionally. Gradually add remaining 2 tablespoons flour and the remaining ¼ teaspoon salt, stirring until mushrooms are coated. Gradually stir in cream. Cook 1 minute or until thickened and smooth, stirring constantly. Divide filling among tart shells. Arrange tarts in 13×9×2-inch pan. Bake in preheated 350°F oven 5 minutes or until hot. Garnish as desired. Makes 22 appetizers.

Crisp Vegetables with Clam Dip

Crisp Vegetables with Clam Dip

     1 package (3 ounces) cream
        cheese, softened
     ½ cup mayonnaise
     ½ cup dairy sour cream
     2 tablespoons minced chives
     2 tablespoons minced parsley
     1 can (10 ounces) whole baby
        clams, well drained
        Assorted vegetables for dippers

Beat cream cheese in medium bowl until fluffy. Beat in mayonnaise, sour cream, chives and parsley. Stir in clams. Serve with assorted vegetables. Makes 1½ cups.

Halakahiki Sausage

     1 pound smoky-link sausage,
        lightly browned
     1 can (8 ounces) DOLE® Crushed
        Pineapple in Syrup
     1 jar (10 ounces) peach
        preserves, apricot jam or
        orange marmalade
     1 jar (6 ounces) prepared mustard

Cut sausages diagonally into bite-sized pieces. Combine undrained pineapple, preserves and mustard in small saucepan; cook over low heat 5 minutes. Add sausage and simmer 15 minutes more. Transfer mixture to chafing dish. Serve hot. Makes 10 servings.

FESTIVE DRINKS

Hot Holiday Punch

    1 cup granulated sugar
    ½ cup packed brown sugar
    4 cups apple cider
    1 cinnamon stick
    12 whole cloves
    2 cups Florida Grapefruit Juice
    2 cups Florida Orange Juice
    Orange slices
    Maraschino cherry halves
      (optional)
    Whole cloves (optional)

Combine sugars and apple cider in large saucepan. Heat over medium heat, stirring until sugars dissolve. Add cinnamon stick and cloves. Bring to a boil over medium heat. Reduce heat to low; simmer 5 minutes. Add grapefruit and orange juice. Heat, but do not boil. Strain into heatproof punch bowl. Garnish with orange slices decorated with maraschino cherry halves and whole cloves. Serve in heatproof punch cups. Makes 8 (8-ounce) servings.

Favorite recipe from **Florida Department of Citrus**

Tropical Island Punch

2 cans (6 ounces each) frozen
    pineapple juice concentrate,
    thawed
1 can (6 ounces) frozen limeade
    concentrate, thawed
1 can (6 ounces) frozen orange
    juice concentrate, thawed
9¾ cups water
2 cups DOMINO® SuperFine
    Sugar
3 bottles (12 ounces each)
    ginger ale, chilled
    Ice
    Maraschino cherries
    Pineapple slices
1 banana, cut into slices
    Lime slices

Combine concentrates in large
container. Add water and sugar. Stir
until sugar dissolves. Refrigerate,
covered, until chilled. Add ginger ale.
Pour over ice in punch bowl. With
wooden picks, attach maraschino
cherries to centers of pineapple slices.
Float pineapple, banana and lime
slices on punch. Makes about 28
(5-ounce) servings.

Hot Holiday Punch

Mimosa Cocktail

1 bottle (750 mL) champagne, chilled
3 cups Florida Orange Juice, chilled

Combine equal parts of champagne and orange juice in champagne glasses. Serve immediately. Makes 12 servings.

Favorite recipe from **Florida Department of Citrus**

Eggless Nog

⅓ cup instant nonfat milk powder
½ teaspoon rum extract
¼ teaspoon vanilla
1 cup ice cubes and water
Dash nutmeg (optional)

Combine milk powder, rum extract, vanilla and ice cubes and water in blender. Cover and process until ice melts. Pour into tall glass. Sprinkle with nutmeg. Makes 1 serving.

Rosy Apple Punch

1 package (3 ounces) cherry flavored gelatin
1 cup hot LUCKY LEAF® Apple Juice
3 cups cold LUCKY LEAF® Apple Juice
2 tablespoons lemon juice
1 bottle (10 ounces) ginger ale

Dissolve gelatin in hot apple juice in medium bowl. Add cold apple juice and lemon juice. Mix well. Stir in ginger ale. Ladle in punch cups. Makes about 8 (5-ounce) servings.

Mimosa Cocktail

Hot Pineapple-Cranberry Sip

Kahlúa® Party Punch

2 cups KAHLÚA®, chilled
1 can (12 ounces) frozen apple
**   juice concentrate, thawed**
½ cup lemon juice, chilled
**   Small chunk ice**
1 bottle (25¼ ounces) sparkling
**   apple juice, chilled**
1 bottle (32 ounces) club soda or
**   lemon-lime soda, chilled**
1 bottle (750 mL) dry champagne,
**   chilled**
1 lemon, thinly sliced
1 small orange, thinly sliced

Combine KAHLÚA®, apple juice
concentrate and lemon juice in
medium bowl. Pour over chunk ice in
punch bowl. Add sparkling apple
juice, then club soda. Add champagne
and stir gently. Garnish with lemon
and orange slices. Makes about 1
gallon, 25 (5-ounce) servings.

Hot Pineapple-Cranberry Sip

2 cups DOLE® Pineapple Juice
2 cups cranberry juice cocktail
¼ cup honey
⅛ teaspoon ground cloves
4 lime slices

Combine juices, honey and cloves in
large saucepan. Bring to a boil over
high heat. Boil 1 minute. Ladle into
heatproof glasses. Garnish with lime
slices. Makes 4 (8-ounce) servings.

Hot Spiced Pineapple

1 can (46 ounces) DOLE®
    Pineapple Juice
1 cup apple juice
½ cup packed light brown sugar
¼ cup butter or margarine
1 teaspoon ground cinnamon
¼ teaspoon ground nutmeg
⅛ teaspoon ground cloves
1 cup light rum

Combine juices, sugar, butter and spices in large saucepan. Simmer 15 minutes over medium-low heat. Pour in rum. Ladle into heatproof glasses. Garnish as desired. Makes 9 (6-ounce) servings.

Frozen Margaritas

½ cup REALIME® Lime Juice from
    Concentrate
½ cup tequila
¼ cup triple sec or other orange-
    flavored liqueur
1 cup powdered sugar
4 cups ice cubes

Combine all ingredients in blender except ice cubes. Cover and blend well. Gradually add ice, blending until smooth. Garnish as desired. Serve immediately. Makes about 1 quart.

Kahlúa® & Eggnog

1 quart dairy eggnog
¾ cup KAHLÚA®
    Whipped cream
    Ground nutmeg

Combine eggnog and KAHLÚA® in 1½-quart pitcher. Pour into punch cups. Top with whipped cream. Sprinkle with nutmeg. Makes about 8 servings.

Wassail Bowl

1 can (20 ounces) DOLE® Chunk
    Pineapple in Syrup
6 baking apples, cored, cut into
    halves
1½ cups sugar, divided
2 cups water, divided
1 teaspoon ground nutmeg
1 teaspoon ground ginger
¼ teaspoon ground mace
6 whole cloves
6 whole allspice
1 cinnamon stick
6 large eggs, separated
1 bottle (750 mL) dry sherry or
    Madeira wine
2 cups brandy

Drain pineapple, reserving syrup. Arrange apples in 3-quart shallow baking pan. Combine ½ cup of the sugar, reserved pineapple syrup and 1 cup of the water. Pour over apples. Bake in 375°F oven 1 hour or until apples are tender. Mix in pineapple.

Meanwhile, combine remaining 1 cup sugar, remaining 1 cup water, the nutmeg, ginger, mace, cloves, allspice and cinnamon stick in small saucepan. Bring to a boil over high heat; boil 5 minutes. Remove from heat. Beat egg whites in large bowl until stiff peaks form. Lightly beat egg yolks in another large bowl. Fold whites into yolks. Strain sugar-spice liquid into eggs. Combine sherry and brandy in medium saucepan. Heat over medium heat just to a simmer. Slowly pour into egg mixture, beating rapidly. Spoon in baked apples and pineapple. Makes about 2 quarts, about 12 (5-ounce) servings.

Hot Spiced Pineapple

Grapefruit Spritzer

Grapefruit Spritzers

**1 can (6 ounces) frozen Florida
    Grapefruit Juice concentrate,
    thawed**
**2¼ cups club soda, chilled
    Fresh strawberries**

Pour grapefruit concentrate into large pitcher. Slowly pour in club soda; mix well. Serve in punch cups. Garnish with strawberries. Makes 4 (6-ounce) servings.

Favorite recipe from Florida Department of Citrus

Hot Spiced Wine

**1 quart water
2 cups sugar
25 whole cloves
3 cinnamon sticks
½ lemon, peeled
1 bottle (1.5 L) CRIBARI®
    Zinfandel**

Combine water, sugar, spices and lemon in medium saucepan. Boil over medium-high heat until mixture is syrupy. Reduce heat to low. Add wine; simmer 5 minutes. Do not let wine boil. Makes about 2½ quarts, about 16 (5-ounce) servings.

Boggs® Cranberry Punch

**1 bottle (750 mL) BOGGS®
    Cranberry Liqueur, chilled**
1 bottle (750 mL) light rum, chilled
**1 bottle (32 ounces) club soda,
    chilled**
**1 cup lemon juice, chilled
    Ice
    Sliced peaches, strawberries
    and oranges**

Combine BOGGS® Cranberry Liqueur, rum, club soda and lemon juice in punch bowl. Add ice. Garnish with fruit. Makes 3 quarts, about 18 (5-ounce) servings.

Spicy Apple Eggnog

    3 cups milk
    2 cups light cream or half and half
    2 eggs, beaten
    ⅓ cup sugar
    ½ teaspoon ground cinnamon
      Dash salt
    ¾ cup apple brandy
      Ground nutmeg

Combine milk, light cream, eggs, sugar, cinnamon and salt in large saucepan. Heat over medium heat until mixture is slightly thickened and heated through, but do not boil. Remove from heat; stir in brandy. To serve, ladle into heatproof glasses or cups. Sprinkle each with nutmeg. Makes 9 (5-ounce) servings.

Favorite recipe from **Wisconsin Milk Marketing Board**⊙

Sunny Champagne Punch

    2 cans (46 ounces each) DOLE®
      Pineapple Juice, chilled
    2 bottles (750 mL) dry
      champagne, chilled
    2 cups chenin blanc wine, chilled
    1 can (20 ounces) DOLE® Chunk
      Pineapple in Juice
      Ice cubes
    1 lemon, thinly sliced
    1 orange, thinly sliced

Combine pineapple juice, champagne, wine and undrained pineapple chunks in large punch bowl. Add ice cubes. Float lemon and orange slices on top. Makes 1½ gallons, about 38 (5-ounce) servings.

Sangria Spritzer

    2 cups boiling water
    6 LIPTON® FLO-THRU® Tea Bags
    1 quart apple cider
    1 bottle (750 mL) dry white wine
    2 cans (6 ounces each) frozen
      orange juice concentrate
    2 cans (6 ounces each) frozen
      lemonade concentrate
    2 bottles (7 ounces each) club
      soda, chilled
      Lemon slices
      Apple slices

Pour boiling water over tea bags in teapot. Cover and brew 5 minutes. Remove tea bags and cool slightly. Combine tea, cider, wine and concentrates in punch bowl. Refrigerate, covered, until chilled. Just before serving, add club soda. Serve with ice and garnish with lemon and apple slices. Makes about 20 (5-ounce) servings.

Hot Jolly Punch Made with Squirt®

    4 cups unsweetened pineapple
      juice
    1½ cups apricot nectar
    1 cup orange juice
    1 bottle (1 L) SQUIRT®
    2 cinnamon sticks
    1 teaspoon whole cloves
    ¼ teaspoon whole cardamom
      seeds, crushed
    10 ounces whiskey (optional)

Combine all ingredients except whiskey in large saucepan. Bring to a boil over high heat. Reduce heat to low; simmer 15 to 20 minutes. Remove pan from heat. Strain into 9 mugs. Add 1 ounce whiskey to each mug. Makes about 10 (8-ounce) servings.

Kahlúa® & Coffee

1½ ounces KAHLÚA®
Hot coffee
Whipped cream (optional)

Pour KAHLÚA® into steaming cup of coffee. Top with whipped cream. Makes 1 serving.

Kahlúa® Hot Spiced Apple Cider

1½ ounces KAHLÚA®
1 cup hot apple cider or apple juice
1 cinnamon stick

Pour KAHLÚA® into hot cider. Stir with cinnamon stick. Makes 1 serving.

Top to bottom: Kahlúa® Hot Spiced Apple Cider, Kahlúa® Parisian Coffee, Kahlúa® & Coffee

Kahlúa® Parisian Coffee

1 ounce cognac or brandy
½ ounce KAHLÚA®
½ ounce Grand Marnier
  Hot coffee
  Whipped cream
  Orange peel (optional)

Pour cognac, KAHLÚA® and Grand Marnier into steaming cup of coffee. Top with whipped cream. Garnish with orange peel. Makes 1 serving.

Skiers' Glögg

4 whole cardamom pods or
  24 cardamom seeds
¼ cup broken cinnamon stick
25 whole cloves
  Peel of 1 orange
1 bottle (1.5 L) port, divided
1 bottle (1.5 L) CRIBARI®
  Zinfandel, divided
1½ cups raisins
1 cup whole blanched almonds
2 cups cubed sugar
1 bottle (750 mL) brandy, divided

Combine cardamom, cinnamon, cloves and orange peel on double thickness of cheesecloth. Bring edges of cheesecloth together; tie with cotton string. Combine ½ of the port and ½ of the Zinfandel and the raisins in large saucepan. Add spice bag. Bring to a boil over high heat; reduce heat to low. Simmer, covered, 15 to 20 minutes.

Add remaining wines and the almonds; continue heating. Place sugar cubes in another large saucepan; set aside. Warm ⅓ of the brandy in small saucepan over low heat. Pour over sugar cubes and flame it with a match. When sugar has dissolved and the flame goes out, add the sugar mixture to the wine-spice mixture. Pour in the remaining brandy. Serve drink warm. Makes 20 (8-ounce) servings.

Spiced Tea Refresher

2 cups boiling water
2 tea bags
2 cinnamon sticks
1 bottle (24 ounces) or 3 cups
  WELCH'S® White Grape Juice
2 tablespoons lemon juice
  Ice
4 lemon peel twists

Pour water over tea bags in 2-quart heatproof pitcher. Add cinnamon sticks and steep for 5 minutes. Remove and discard tea bags and cinnamon sticks. Stir in WELCH'S® White Grape Juice and lemon juice. Pour over ice in tall glasses. Serve with lemon twists. Makes 4 servings.

Fish House Punch

2 cups KARO® Dark Corn Syrup
2 cups water
2 tablespoons grated lemon peel
⅔ cup lemon juice
2 cups light rum
1 cup brandy
½ cup peach brandy
  Crushed ice

Combine corn syrup and water in 3-quart saucepan. Bring to a boil over medium heat, stirring occasionally. Stir in lemon peel and juice. Remove from heat. Cool. Stir in rum and brandies. Pour over crushed ice in punch bowl. Makes about 2 quarts, 10 (5-ounce) servings.

THE DESSERT BAR

Walnut Apple Tarts

- ¾ cup all-purpose flour
  Sugar
- 6 tablespoons cold butter or margarine, cut into small pieces
- 1 to 1½ tablespoons water
- 2 large tart apples, pared, cored
  Juice of 1 lemon
- ¼ cup currant jelly, melted
- ½ cup finely chopped toasted walnuts
  Butter or margarine, melted

Combine flour and 1 tablespoon of sugar in medium bowl. Cut in butter until mixture resembles coarse meal. Stir in water (mixture will be crumbly). Turn onto lightly floured surface; knead lightly to form a ball. Flatten; wrap in plastic wrap. Refrigerate 20 minutes. Roll out dough on lightly floured surface into 12-inch circle, about ¼ inch thick. Cut out 7 to 8 circles, about 4½ inches in diameter. Crimp edges. Arrange on baking sheet; refrigerate.

Slice apples ¼ inch thick. Drizzle

with lemon juice. Brush each pastry circle with jelly. Sprinkle with ½ of the nuts, dividing equally. Arrange overlapping apple slices on each circle. Sprinkle with remaining nuts. Drizzle with melted butter; sprinkle with additional sugar. Bake in preheated 425°F oven 15 to 18 minutes or until apples are tender when tested with a fork. Makes 7 to 8 tarts.

Favorite recipe from **Walnut Marketing Board**

Pictured above: Walnut Apple Tarts, Chocolate Walnut Macaroons (page 86), Viennese Chocolate (page 87)

Take-Along Applesauce Cake

1½ cups **WHEAT CHEX® Brand Cereal**
1 jar (16 ounces) applesauce
2 large eggs, beaten
2 teaspoons vanilla, divided
1 cup granulated sugar
½ cup vegetable shortening
1½ cups all-purpose flour
1 tablespoon baking powder
1½ teaspoons ground cinnamon
½ teaspoon salt
½ teaspoon baking soda
1 cup raisins
3 cups sifted powdered sugar
¼ cup butter or margarine, softened
2 tablespoons milk

Grease 13×9×2-inch baking pan. Combine cereal, applesauce, eggs and 1 teaspoon of the vanilla in medium bowl; mix well. Let stand 5 minutes. Stir to break up cereal. Cream sugar and shortening in large bowl. Stir in applesauce mixture, mixing well. Stir in flour, baking powder, cinnamon, salt and baking soda until well combined. Stir in raisins. Spread in prepared pan. Bake in preheated 350°F oven 35 to 40 minutes or until cake tester inserted in center comes out clean. Cool in pan on wire rack. Beat powdered sugar and butter in large bowl. Stir in remaining 1 teaspoon vanilla and the milk; mix well. Spread over cake. Garnish as desired. Makes 12 servings.

Chocolate Walnut Macaroons

- 3 cups ground toasted walnuts
- 1 cup plus 2 tablespoons sugar
- 3 egg whites
- ½ cup unsweetened cocoa powder
- 1 teaspoon maple flavoring
  Chopped toasted walnuts or chocolate sprinkles for toppings

Combine walnuts, sugar, egg whites, cocoa and maple flavoring in large bowl until well blended. Drop by generous tablespoonfuls onto greased cookie sheets. Sprinkle with toppings. Bake in preheated 350°F oven 20 minutes or until just set. Centers will be soft. Remove to wire rack to cool. Store in airtight container. Makes about 2 dozen cookies.

Favorite recipe from **Walnut Marketing Board**

Viennese Chocolate

- ½ cup chopped walnuts
- ¾ cup unsweetened cocoa powder
- 1 teaspoon instant coffee powder
- 1 cup boiling water
- ½ cup KAHLÚA®
- ¾ cup butter
- ¼ cup vegetable shortening
- 1¾ cups sugar
- 5 large eggs
- 1 teaspoon vanilla
- 2 cups sifted all-purpose flour
- 1½ teaspoons baking soda
- ¼ teaspoon baking powder
- 1 teaspoon salt
  Kahlúa® Glaze (recipe follows)
  Kahlúa® Fudge Frosting (recipe follows)
  Kahlúa® Cream (see page 88)

Line bottom of two 9-inch round baking pans with baking parchment or waxed paper. Butter paper and sides of pan. Sprinkle walnuts evenly over paper; set aside.

Combine cocoa and coffee in small bowl. Pour in boiling water; stir until smooth. Add KAHLÚA® and cool. Cream butter, shortening, sugar, eggs and vanilla in large bowl until fluffy and sugar is dissolved. Resift flour with baking soda, baking powder and salt into medium bowl. Alternately beat dry ingredients and chocolate mixture into butter mixture. Divide batter between prepared pans. Bake in preheated 350°F oven 25 to 30 minutes or until top springs back when touched lightly in center.

Cool in pans on wire rack 5 minutes. Turn out onto wire racks. Remove paper liners; cool completely. Meanwhile, prepare Kahlúa® Glaze, Kahlúa® Fudge Frosting and Kahlúa® Cream.

Split each layer in half horizontally. Brush 3 of the layers with Kahlúa® Glaze. Spread each of the 3 layers with 2 tablespoons of the Kahlúa® Fudge Frosting, then the Kahlúa® Cream. Stack the 3 layers. Place fourth layer on top. Spread remaining Kahlúa® Frosting over sides and top. Garnish as desired. Makes 12 servings.

Kahlúa® Glaze: Heat 3 tablespoons KAHLÚA® and 3 tablespoons red currant jelly in small saucepan over low heat until jelly is melted.

Kahlúa® Fudge Frosting: Combine 6 squares (1 ounce each) semisweet chocolate, ¾ cup butter or margarine, ¼ cup KAHLÚA®, ¼ cup whipping cream and 1 teaspoon vanilla in medium saucepan. Heat over medium heat until smooth, stirring frequently. Remove from heat. Blend in 2½ cups sifted powdered sugar. Beat until frosting cools and just begins to hold its shape.

Kahlúa® Chiffon Mince Pie

1 envelope unflavored gelatine
⅓ cup sugar, divided
¼ teaspoon salt
2 large eggs, separated
1 cup half and half
¼ cup KAHLÚA®
¾ cup prepared mincemeat
½ cup whipping cream
1 baked (9-inch) pie shell
Kahlúa® Cream (recipe follows)
Sliced unblanched almonds
(optional)

Combine gelatine, about ½ of the sugar and the salt in top of double boiler. Beat egg yolks with half and half in small bowl; stir into gelatine mixture. Place pan over simmering water and cook, stirring frequently, until custard thickens slightly and coats back of spoon. Combine KAHLÚA® and mincemeat in small bowl; add to custard. Remove from heat; cool. Then place pan in ice water bath to chill mixture until it begins to jell. Beat egg whites in a narrow bowl until fine foam forms. Gradually beat in remaining sugar until stiff peaks form. Beat cream in another narrow bowl until stiff peaks form. Gently fold meringue, then cream into jelled mixture until blended. Turn into baked shell and lightly swirl top. Refrigerate, loosely covered, until firm. Pipe Kahlúa® Cream about 1 inch from outside edge of pie with rosette tip. Garnish with almonds. Makes 8 servings.

Kahlúa® Cream: Beat ½ cup whipping cream and 1 tablespoon KAHLÚA® in narrow bowl until stiff. Makes about 1 cup.

Mini Mincemeat Tarts

1 can (20 ounces) DOLE®
   Crushed Pineapple in Syrup
2 cups prepared mincemeat
½ cup toasted slivered almonds
1 teaspoon ground allspice
3 cups all-purpose flour
2 tablespoons sugar
¼ teaspoon salt
¾ cup butter or margarine
½ cup cold water
1 egg yolk
1 tablespoon light cream

Drain pineapple well, pressing out syrup with back of spoon. Combine pineapple, mincemeat, almonds and allspice in medium bowl; set aside. Combine flour, sugar and salt in another medium bowl. Cut in butter until mixture resembles coarse meal. Add enough water to form ball. Divide dough into 12 pieces. Roll out 6 pieces on lightly floured surface and fit into 3¾-inch tart tins. Spoon pineapple mixture into each. Roll out remaining 6 pieces of dough. Cover each tart; flute edges. Make slits on top. Decorate as desired with dough scraps. Combine egg yolk and cream in small bowl. Brush over tops of tarts. Bake in preheated 375°F oven 20 minutes. Reduce heat to 350°F; bake 20 minutes more. Makes 6 tarts.

Mini Mincemeat Tarts

Pumpkin Trifle

1 pound cake (1-pound size)
6 tablespoons orange juice
1 cup (14-ounce jar) cranberry-
     orange relish
3 cups whipping cream
¾ cup sifted powdered sugar
2 cups LIBBY'S® Pumpkin Pie Mix
1 cup sliced almonds

Cut pound cake into 12 slices.
Sprinkle cake slices with orange juice;
spread with cranberry-orange relish.
Beat whipping cream and powdered
sugar in large bowl until stiff peaks
form. Fold pumpkin pie mix into
whipped cream. Arrange 4 of the cake
slices on bottom of trifle bowl. Top
with 3 cups of the pumpkin-whipped
cream mixture. Top with ⅓ cup of the
sliced almonds . Repeat layers 2 more
times. Cover loosely. Refrigerate
several hours or overnight. Garnish
as desired. Makes 12 servings.

Pumpkin Nut Pound Cake

¾ cup granulated sugar
½ cup packed light brown sugar
¾ cup butter or margarine,
     softened
2 large eggs
1 cup LIBBY'S® Solid Pack
     Pumpkin
1¾ cups all-purpose flour
½ cup finely chopped or ground
     pecans
1 teaspoon baking soda
½ teaspoon salt
1½ teaspoons ground cinnamon
½ teaspoon ground allspice
¼ teaspoon ground nutmeg
1 cup sifted powdered sugar
3 to 4 teaspoons water
     Sliced almonds (optional)

Top: Pumpkin Trifle
Bottom: Pumpkin Nut Pound Cake

Grease and flour 9×5-inch loaf pan. Combine sugars, butter and eggs in large bowl. Beat until fluffy. Add pumpkin; beat just until blended. Combine flour, pecans, baking soda, salt and spices in medium bowl. Gradually add to batter, beating well after each addition. Pour into prepared pan. Bake at 325°F 75 to 80 minutes or until cake tester inserted in center comes out clean. Cool cake in pan on wire rack 10 minutes. Remove from pan and cool completely on wire rack. Combine powdered sugar and water in medium bowl. Drizzle over cake. Garnish with almonds. Makes 1 large loaf.

Plum Pudding Pie

½ cup golden raisins
½ cup chopped pitted dates
⅓ cup chopped candied cherries
⅓ cup KAHLÚA®
½ cup chopped walnuts
⅓ cup dark corn syrup
½ teaspoon pumpkin pie spice
¼ cup butter or margarine, softened
¼ cup packed brown sugar
2 tablespoons all-purpose flour
¼ teaspoon salt
2 large eggs, slightly beaten
1 unbaked (9-inch) pastry shell
Kahlúa® Cream (see page 88)

Combine raisins, dates, cherries and KAHLÚA® in large bowl. Let stand 1 hour or longer to blend flavors. Add walnuts, corn syrup and pumpkin pie spice. Cream butter, brown sugar, flour and salt in medium bowl. Stir in eggs, then blend into fruit mixture. Transfer to pastry shell. Bake in preheated 350°F oven, on first rack below oven center, 35 minutes or just until filling is set and crust is golden. Cool on wire rack. Prepare Kahlúa® Cream. To serve, pipe Kahlúa® Cream around edge of pie using rosette tip. Garnish as desired. Makes 8 servings.

Plum Pudding Pie

Goody-Goody Logs

4 cups BRAN CHEX® Brand
    Cereal, crushed to make
    2 cups
1 cup dried apples, finely
    chopped
¾ cup dates, finely chopped
¾ cup flaked coconut, divided
½ cup chopped nuts
1 package (3¾ ounces) instant
    vanilla pudding and pie filling
    mix
⅓ cup light corn syrup
2 tablespoons lemon juice

Combine cereal, apples, dates, ½ cup
of the coconut and the nuts in large
bowl. Combine pudding mix, corn
syrup and lemon juice in small bowl;
mix well. Pour over fruit mixture,
stirring to coat all pieces. Form batter
into two 8-inch rolls (about 1½ inches
in diameter). Coat fruit rolls with
remaining ¼ cup coconut. Wrap each
roll in waxed paper. Refrigerate 2 to 3
hours. To serve, cut into ¼-inch
slices. Makes about 64 slices.

Pecan Pumpkin Pie

3 large eggs, slightly beaten
1 cup sugar
½ cup dark corn syrup
1 cup LIBBY'S® Solid Pack
    Pumpkin
1 tablespoon vanilla
1 cup pecan halves
1 unbaked (9-inch) pastry shell

Combine eggs, sugar, corn syrup,
pumpkin and vanilla in medium bowl.
Gently stir in pecans. Pour into
pastry shell. Bake in preheated 375°F
oven 55 to 60 minutes or until knife
inserted halfway between center and
edge comes out clean. Makes about 8
servings.

Kahlúa® Fantasy Chocolate Cheesecake

Chocolate Crumb Crust (recipe
    follows)
1½ cups semisweet chocolate
    pieces
¼ cup KAHLÚA®
2 tablespoons butter or margarine
2 large eggs, beaten
⅓ cup sugar
¼ teaspoon salt
1 cup dairy sour cream
2 packages (8 ounces each)
    cream cheese, softened

Prepare Chocolate Crumb Crust.
Place chocolate, KAHLÚA® and
butter in heavy, small saucepan. Heat
over medium heat until chocolate
melts; stir until smooth. Set aside.

Combine eggs, sugar and salt in large
bowl. Add sour cream; blend well.
Add cream cheese; beat until smooth.
Gradually blend in chocolate mixture.
Pour into prepared crust. Bake in
preheated 350°F oven 40 minutes or
until filling is barely set in center. Let
stand on wire rack 1 hour at room
temperature. Refrigerate, loosely
covered, several hours or overnight.
Garnish as desired. Makes 12 to 14
servings.

Chocolate Crumb Crust: Combine 1⅓
cups chocolate wafer crumbs, ¼ cup
softened butter or margarine and 1
tablespoon sugar in medium bowl.
Press firmly in bottom of 9-inch
springform pan.

Acknowledgments

American Egg Board
Bel Paese Sales Co., Inc.
Best Foods (Best Foods Real
    Mayonnaise, Hellmann's Real
    Mayonnaise and Karo Corn Syrup)
Borden, Inc.
Chex® brand cereals, Ralston Purina
    Company
Cribari & Sons Winery
Crisco® Oil
Domino® Sugar, Amstar Sugar
    Corporation, New York, NY
Dole® Food Company
Florida Department of Citrus
Heublein, Inc.

Knouse Foods, Inc.
Knox® Unflavored Gelatine
Libby, Division of Carnation
    Company
Lipton® Flo-Thru® Tea Bags
Lipton® Recipe Soup Mixes
Maidstone Wine & Spirits Inc.
National Live Stock and Meat Board
National Pork Producers Council
Squirtco, Inc., a division of A&W
    Brands, Inc., White Plains, NY
Walnut Marketing Board©
Welch's®
Wisconsin Milk Marketing Board©
Wish-Bone® Dressings

Picture Credits

American Egg Board, page 36
Bel Paese Sales Co., Inc., page 6
Best Foods (Best Foods Real
    Mayonnaise and Hellmann's Real
    Mayonnaise), page 22
Chex® brand cereals, Ralston Purina
    Company, pages 40, 51, 54, 69, 72,
    86
Crisco® Oil, pages 7, 63
Dole® Food Company, pages 41, 50,
    52, 66, 73, 77, 79, 89, Back Cover
    (bottom left)
Florida Department of Citrus,
    pages 76, 80
Knox® Unflavored Gelatine, page 62

Libby, Division of Carnation
    Company, pages 12, 28, 90
Lipton® Recipe Soup Mixes,
    pages 55, 62
Maidstone Wine & Spirits Inc.,
    pages 82, 91
National Live Stock and Meat Board,
    pages 20, 21, 31, 44, 49, 57, 67,
    Front Cover (bottom left), Back
    Cover (top right)
National Pork Producers Council,
    pages 4, 17
Wisconsin Milk Marketing Board,©
    pages 27, 35, 61
Wish-Bone® Dressings, page 64

INDEX